Organize
or Die

Organize or Die

Business, Marketing
and Communications
Strategies for
Labor Leaders, Agents
and Organizers

Mark Breslin

McAlly International Press
CASTRO VALLEY, CALIFORNIA

1st printing 2003   3rd printing 2005
2nd printing 2004   4th printing 2005

ISBN-10   0-9741662-3-5
ISBN-13   978-0-9741662-3-0
LCCN 2003107646

Table of Contents

v

For my daughter Ally.

Acknowledgments

This book would not have been possible without the guidance, support and belief of a number of special people and organizations. I would like to thank the incredible team of people that have worked with and for me at the Engineering and Utility Contractors Association (EUCA) over these many years. This includes the many contractors, labor representatives and staff members who have worked so hard at making cooperation and mutual interest their way of doing business. Special thanks go to Leslie Lord for her 20 years of remarkable efforts on behalf of me and EUCA, as well as Kelly Montes for her keen editing eye. Also I would have not been bold enough to try something different without the encouragement and guidance of my many mentors who, each in their own way, share in any success I may have in my professional life. Some of them include Mike Fuller, Gary Andrews, Dean Rasmussen, Rich Gates, Jim Dalton, Dan Lowry, and Paul Aherne.

I'd also like to thank my mom for my belief in myself. My father for passing on his business acumen. My step-dad for showing me how to care first and ask questions later. My special thanks to my fiancee Susan for using love, encouragement and pointed humor to push me to my best effort. And to my entire family for helping to remind me that we are all part of something greater than the world of business and ambition.

INTRODUCTION

The Management S.O.B.

I may have my faults, but being wrong ain't one of them.
—JIMMY HOFFA

I am a management S.O.B.

I have been threatened, picketed, spit at, defamed, sued, harassed and generally made to feel unloved. I represent employers in terminations, sexual harassment, strikes, lockouts, jurisdictional disputes and other sudden death games. My winning arbitration record is Cy Young quality. My Italian and Irish bloodlines cause occasional loud and unruly outbursts. I have broken phones but never promises. When provoked, I can laugh it off or froth like a junkyard dog.

I have taken an eye for an eye, gone nose to nose and matched drink for drink. I have no formal legal training but I can find the obscure contract loophole. I have no guilt about using choke-chain lawyers to bare fangs at labor union dinosaurs. I confess to have just recently given up the amusing pastime of "taunt the first year business agent."

I am, by trade or situation, a negotiator, mediator, father confessor and sympathetic arm twister. Yes, I am a management S.O.B. But at the same time, I have been honored by local and international unions. I have conducted seminars for thousands of business managers, agents and organizers across the United States. I was even the recipient of one of the highest honors granted by an International Union. As a result, I now own more plaques, watches, pins, jackets and pens with union logos than I will ever need or use.

You see, despite my obvious lack of charm and my many serious character flaws, I am a very successful union organizer. I am a wolf in wolf's clothing. It's just that I selectively promote and eat the sheep.

Results speak louder than words. One District Council used the ideas contained in this book and signed up several hundred new companies on a top-down basis in three years—no salting, campaigns or votes required. I have personally brokered relationships and contracts between more than 100 non-union companies and various unions in the past seven years. We should all have such productive hobbies.

Now before you finger me as a college "suit" or heartless corporate kill-shot type, without an understanding of an honest day's work, a little history is in order. I started working when I was 12. To put myself through high school and college, I would do almost anything for money. I've been a paperboy, busboy, waiter, fry-cook, house painter, drywaller, janitor, bar-back, retail clerk, pump jockey, laborer, carpenter, foreman, production manager, and the list goes on and on. I've been paid union, non-union and cash under the table. I've had dirt on my jeans. Mud on my boots. Dust up my nose. Paint in my hair. Whatever it took. A man apart from "an honest day's work?" Hardly. Been there and done that.

I come from three generations of contracting. My great grandfather, grandfather and step-dad were all contractors. By age 26 I had put myself through college, and rapidly become the chief executive of a contractors trade association in California. And, without knowing it, I became the youngest S.O.B. in the nation with this job. I knew nothing, acted like it and didn't know any better.

It was then, with a lot of help from some class-act labor leaders and innovative employers, that I began to formulate a different way of conducting labor-management relations. Cooperation and mutual interest began to govern my working relationships with my union counterparts.

As a result of this approach, applied over two decades, the association tripled in size. It became a leading multi-employer bargaining unit and an innovator in labor-management relations in California. The unit currently represents more than two hundred major companies. These companies employ thousands of union workers, for millions of man-hours each year, with billions of dollars in secured contracts.

So why now, at the pinnacle of management S.O.B. success, might I compromise my management credibility by becoming known as a "union organizer"? What could I possibly gain by promoting relationships between non-union firms and organized labor?

My motives are not noble. I am not engaged in a fight for the heart and soul of the American worker. The simple fact is that I represent unionized employers and it is easier to teach market recovery strategies to union leaders, agents and organizers than it is to get them to modify outdated contracts or accept wage, fringe or work rule concessions the members will scream about .

Thus, I am using nontraditional strategies to aggressively expand union market share. In fact, I am teaching labor to increase market share and, as a result, even the playing field for my employers at the same time. Is this a marketing innovation? Maybe. Is this the new labor-management dynamic at work? Perhaps. But the blunt truth is that it is a survival technique for existing union employers. This market is governed by a harsh economic and political environment that does not measure itself by its ideology. It's dog-eat-dog determined by price, performance and results. It's the American Way.

I have no time to debate the moral merits or deficiencies of this system. But I have invested nearly a decade devising very specific marketing and business development strategies to thrive within it. This book is designed to address top-down organizing, marketing and business development strategies up to, and including, closing the sale on non-union employers. It's also about conducting yourself as a professional labor representative in the business world.

This book does not address bottom-up techniques such as salting, arm twisting or ass chewing. Someone else will teach you those strategies, essential for some campaigns, but not my style. To me, most business relationships starting that way will probably lack the trust, loyalty and mutual benefit that is the foundation for any long-term relationship. I know that sometimes you "gotta-do-what-you-gotta-do"—but what if you didn't have to go to that extreme to begin with?

So, as you read this book, keep an open mind. The following pages may not always be easy to accept or digest. But you may find, in its raw and vulgar nature, some compelling in-your-face truths; like a nasty car accident you just can't look away from. One guarantee is that if you are willing to try something different, there is at least one thing in the pages ahead that will change the way you do business.

CHAPTER 1

Organize or Die

There is a point at which everything becomes simple and there is no choice, because all will be lost if you look back. It is the point of no return.

—DAG HAMMARSKJOLD

Organize or Die

Organize or Die is not a threat or a slogan. It is a simple choice and the clock is ticking. It may seem melodramatic, but it summarizes your task as organized labor. You have let your market share slip away over decades of complacency and arrogance. Now you must regain it. To do so in a manner that will bring meaningful percentages back to the unionized sector, you must organize. If you do not, you risk becoming truly insignificant; you risk the death of your relevance to American business and commerce. Across vast stretches of this nation, labor, as measured by market share, has already died. As such, it will take a long time to regain what you have lost. If labor seriously considers its future, then "Organize or Die" may not seem overly dramatic—but simply a logical conclusion…and a call for action.

The Objective: Market Recovery

This book is about regaining union market share. It outlines, in some detail, specific business development strategies and tactics for union leaders. The ideas and concepts presented may be quite foreign and unfamiliar. This is for good reason. As labor unions attempt to recapture lost market share and to re-energize organizing efforts, they are going back to their historical roots. These roots are exhibited in programs and strategies such as salting, COMET and other bottom-up organizing efforts. While I recognize that for some employers, whose minds and doors are completely closed, these activities may be the only alternative, but it is not universally the best approach.

Hard-core tactics such as these were the hallmark of labor's early organizing efforts. They reflect a strategy that assumes that everyone needs to be forced to make a decision. Frankly, I believe that labor is again turning to these strategies because it is the tried and true methodology—it is all that you know. Labor has never put significant time, resources or manpower into professional business development on a comparable level with most American business models.

This "play hardball" philosophy often extends beyond strategy and becomes both a mentality and value system. This value system can become an organizational approach that extends from union leaders down to rank-and-file. Over time, this way of thinking leaves no room for marketing strategies designed for partnering with employers or creating top-down organizing success. Labor is investing nearly all of its resources in programs that attempt to force employers to become unionized. I believe this is a strategic mistake.

This book provides an alternative, one that emphasizes proven principles used by nearly every other business enterprise in America. These principles are based on market analysis, client needs, value, and return-on-investment. An opportunity exists to make dramatic and positive changes in the manner in which firms become unionized. I have seen it. And so have the unions I have worked with, by signing up hundreds and hundreds of companies.

Helpful Definitions

There are a few definitions that need to be explained right off the bat. You will note that I use the terms "organizing" and "business development" interchangeably. To me, they are one and the same.

I use the term "client" for both your existing signatory and non-union targeted employers. They are and always will be clients, and I'll explain why, soon. Market share is the percentage of companies you do business with versus the overall universe of companies you *could* do business with. "Union leader" is a term I use to describe anyone in organized labor in a position to effect, promote or influence policy or change. This is often based more on vision and communication skills than it is on position or title.

I also use the male tense as a descriptor. Forgive me for not being politically correct with all of you fine Democrats (and closet Republicans).

CHAPTER 2

Top-Down Organizing Basics

An invasion of armies can be
resisted, but not an idea whose
time has come.
—VICTOR HUGO

Organizing:
A Business Transaction

Organizing should be considered at its most basic definition, a form of business transaction. It should not be thought of as a mission, crusade or holy war. It is a business transaction where one party is offering services in the form of a long-term, non-guaranteed contract to another party. It is incumbent on the party making this offer to consider the needs, concerns, worries, questions, problems and challenges of the prospective client. Upon addressing these, a sale is made and the parties begin an operational and contractual relationship that usually extends over a period of many years. Organizing is a business transaction. Don't forget this basic premise.

Breslin's 80/20 Rule

As we begin, I would like to emphasize that I am not conceptually opposed to bottom-up organizing. I simply have developed a formula that illustrates the need for a significant focus on top-down organizing strategies. Breslin's 80/20 Rule is as follows:

- ■ In a very positive market, a union could expect (at very best) to organize 80 percent of the available companies on a top-down basis. (I have seen this done.) The other 20 percent would be organized via bottom-up or written off.

- ■ In a very tough market, a union could expect to organize (at very best) only 20 percent of the available companies on a top-down basis. The other 80 percent must be done on a bottom-up basis or written off.

In either case, both methods need to be used. In both markets, there are opportunities for top-down organizing. A general assumption that the market on a whole is either one or the other is a mistake. But, in my view, a minimum of one out of five employers you approach is a decent prospect for a top-down business development approach.

Two Worlds Collide

To be a great organizer you must understand the basic differences between the union and employer community so you can bridge the gap between them. The gap that neither side usually recognizes is the real clash of value systems that occurs between labor and management. These value systems determine how decisions are made, objectives are established, people are hired and success is defined. The differences are described below:

In the employer community, there is a set of laws that dictate who survives and who dies—similar to Darwin's "survival of the fittest." These laws are based on economics and risk. You must always remember the employer is the one taking on 100 percent of the risk. The consequences of their failure can be devastating and total. Many employers still have risk-anxiety behavior driving them long after they have "made it" in their respective industries.

You must understand that the unforgiving nature of the market, economy and competition create the framework of how an employer views the world. Their version of black and white thinking is "Will X (representing anyone or anything being evaluated as a part of their business strategy) help me or hurt me in my economic survival?" It is not about "doing the right thing," "carrying on in the American way" or any other philosophical issues. Simply put, it is about self-preservation and making money. It is not that they are heartless cruel bastards (though some are), it is just that they usually have all of their assets and personal identity tied up in their businesses. As a result, they will do anything necessary to promote or protect their interests. Success is defined in economic terms.

On the flip side is labor. Labor takes no risk in the formula. Labor has no assets at risk and no personal downside in the event of failure. Unions, although concerned with economics as an engine of employment for their members, are political in nature. The survival of the fittest is based on political skills. It is about power and leverage, alliances and betrayals—a chess match of wits, guts and determination. If employers are responding to the external forces of their markets, then unions, on the other hand, are more often responding to the internal forces of their politics. Success is defined in political terms.

This difference creates a huge gap of understanding between the parties. It's not just the usual labor-management debate over who gets a bigger piece of the pie—it is a fundamental difference in organizational cultures—like the Japanese and the Italians trying to cut a business deal without interpreters.

Most of the union representatives I deal with have no understanding of the complications and risks of running a business. Most of the employers I know have not the slightest idea of the political challenges of working in a union. Am I getting around to a moral here? Employers will never see the business world through your eyes. They simply do not care what your issues and problems are. It will not get onto their radar screen. On the other hand, it is vital that you understand as much as possible about the employer's issues, challenges, problems and risks. And further, you need to care about these and respond to them. When labor doesn't care, the employer seeks other alternatives.

I know it sounds one-sided, because it is. The employer is too occupied to see a broader picture. But just remember that his bottom line is driven by the bottom line of his business. Make a study of the employer's organizational culture. Try to cultivate a better understanding of why he does what he does. Spend time with retired employers in your industry, learning all that you can about the strange habits, thoughts and priorities of employers. If you want to be a business partner of choice, this investment of time is necessary.

The Dysfunctional Marriage

Not many "made-in-heaven" marriages look or sound like this labor-management arrangement. But I think that "made in heaven" stuff is unrealistic anyway. The similarities of a union-employer relationship to your average dysfunctional marriage are strikingly familiar:

■ Usually very long-term relationship

■ Restrictive contract with nonspecific terms

■ No layoffs

■ One partner with greater influence than the other

■ Take each other for granted (often)

■ Wish the other would change

■ Hate cleaning up the other's messes

- Don't often discuss meaningful issues
- Respect each other (usually)
- Tolerate each other's flaws
- Escalate arguments over little things
- Harbor hurts for a long time
- Too expensive to get a divorce (usually)

Remember, oftentimes when you are organizing, you are trying to get an avowed bachelor to commit for life or damn near it. He knows about the stability and comfort a good marriage can create. He knows about building a long-term relationship with a dependable partner. He knows that he has to give up a lot of freedoms to gain these things. Making a decision of this gravity takes time. Making a commitment like this will affect the employer for decades. So put yourself in his shoes.

A little charm and a slam-bam in the back seat followed by the shotgun wedding is not going to happen.

Top-Down Vs. Bottom-Up

As noted in the Breslin 80/20 Rule, you must use both top-down and bottom-up organizing strategies to be effective. But how do you decide which is best?

A simple strategy is always try top-down first. Always make a sincere and professional effort to cultivate a relationship and present the benefits of your product to the principals of a firm before bringing down the hammer. It is more cost effective. It gives you an opportunity to open a dialogue. It is the first step to creating a relationship (good or bad, you will eventually have some form of relationship). It defies the existing union stereotypes. It is a professional business courtesy.

Why, if you can convince one company owner to do business with you on a top-down basis, would you spend the time, money and effort to convince ten, twenty or one hundred employees on a bottom-up basis? This is the simple operational and economic appeal of the top-down first approach.

As amazing as it seems, there are employers out there that are not fire breathing, worker-exploiting, Wal-Mart shopping, Rush Limbaugh clones. There are actually some (if not many) who have worked an honest day, appreciate candor and may even respond to your logic and persuasion.

Never underestimate the possibility. At least one out of twenty is ready and willing. If you go around him or her, in a hostile manner, your odds drop to one in a thousand. Top down organizing is much easier in many cases. Don't work harder than 100 percent success requires.

Organizing for Bargaining Power

Organizing is the foundation of your bargaining strength. Give your existing union employers market share, competitiveness and profitability, and they will be obliged to give you everything.

Don't sit there at the bargaining table and give them that same old crappy sob story about how your guys won't vote those concessions or that you need this or that. Bring them the competition's head on a platter and they'll give you all the gold in the kingdom.

Key Points on Market Share

- ■ Market share is union power.
- ■ Market share erodes the employer's whining about competitiveness.
- ■ Market share justifies your position.

What would it be like if you had 95 percent market share? How would life be different? You could name your price. You could control your destiny. You could reach new markets. You would be flooded with dues money. You'd have more bargaining power for purchase of benefit plans. You would command respect in the marketplace. When preaching market share to the agents and rank-and-file, these themes should be the core of your message. What is in it for everyone? Control of your own destiny.

CHAPTER 3

Your Product: The Good, Bad and Ugly

Security can only be achieved through constant change; through discarding old ideas that have outlived their usefulness and adapting others to current facts.
—WILLIAM O. DOUGLAS

Think Really Big

Unions are big business. You have a great product line and extensive resources. You maintain massive organizations across America. You service thousands of employers. You represent millions of workers. So why do you often think, act and present your product like mom-and-pop operations?

When comparing unions to major corporations in the United States, it should be very easy (maybe easier for me than you) to see yourselves as the big, vital business enterprises. Consider business managers as CEOs, district or local managers as vice presidents, business agents as middle managers and account representatives. But if you don't see it, no one else will either. Unions are perceived as throwbacks by the business community because they are not often identified as professional, innovative and well-run organizations. I'm pretty sure most of you don't even think of yourselves that way.

Think big. Think of yourselves on par with the biggest and best major service companies in this nation. Think of yourself as a very important part of the organization, of the economy and the business community at large. You are more than you think you are. You are offering a valuable product to American Business. It's time to start acting like it.

Know Your Product's Benefits

When you buy tires, a stereo, a weed whacker or a house, you've got a lot of questions about quality, features, warranties and service. This is the starting point in the process for you to consider buying. It is no different with union business development. You are presenting union labor services to a potential buyer. Are you ready? Right now, stop and fill in the ten blanks below with benefits that the employer will realize by utilizing union labor services.

_____   _____

_____   _____

_____   _____

_____   _____

_____   _____

Could you come up with ten? How about five? Stumped at two? Guess what—no sale. Don't feel bad. At most of my seminars the contractors, agents, organizers and business managers usually come up with an average of five to seven reasons each. This is unacceptable. It is my contention that organized labor does not know its product, nor can it articulate the benefits in a meaningful and professional manner.

Therefore, it is critical that each and every union representative have a fundamental understanding of the specific benefits of your union's services. Every agent should be trained on these benefits the very first day on the job. Here is a comprehensive reference list:

- Productivity
- Safer Workforce
- Less Workers Compensation Costs
- Uniform Benefit Administration
- No Benefit Administration Costs
- Skilled Workforce
- Flexible Workforce Size
- Mobility
- Political Assistance
- Worker Morale
- Profitability
- Business Partnership
- Drug Free Workplace
- Worker Loyalty
- Dispute Resolution Process
- Market Opportunities
- Apprenticeship Programs
- Special Rates and Agreements
- Targeting or Work Preservation Programs
- Promotion
- Worker Retention
- Field Supervisory Personnel

Everyone working for your union should be trained to know these benefits and be capable of communicating them at a fundamental level.

Know Your Product's Weaknesses

Your product is less than perfect. I guess you already knew that. So if you know the problems of being a union employer, be prepared to discuss them. Don't think you're going to be able to hide them or bullshit the employer. Prepare yourself to address them and show that the advantages far outweigh the disadvantages. Do not be blind or unrealistic due to your union commitment.

Try filling in the ten slots below with your product weaknesses (real or perceived in the marketplace) and then compare to the list that follows:

_____   _____

_____   _____

_____   _____

_____   _____

_____   _____

Negative Product Stereotypes

Whenever I present one of my seminars to union leadership, I ask every labor leader in the audience to pretend they are non-union employers. Then I ask them all the reasons they should *not* become unionized. They are never at a loss for a long list. The list generally includes:

- Loss of Control of Business
- Will Increase Costs
- Union Leaders are Impractical
- Fear of the Unknown
- No Economic Value
- Can Never Fire Anyone
- Jurisdictional Disputes
- Strikes and Slowdowns
- Have to Sign with All Crafts
- They Have *No* Benefits for Me
- Heard From Other Union Employers: Bad Deal
- Don't Want Outsiders Meddling
- Will Have More Problems with Employees
- Union Leaders Are Corrupt
- Don't Trust Unions
- Used to Be Union/Had a Bad Experience

We will address many of these in coming chapters, but there is one that needs to be addressed right from the start—the stereotype of the "bad" union or union leader. The negative stereotypes and inaccurate beliefs noted above need to be attacked from the minute you meet a prospective signatory employer.

This one should be obvious. These negative images are powerful and should never be reinforced. Unfortunately, some people (including many employers and yours truly from time to time) are genetically predisposed to be assholes. In approaching a prospective client, don't come on strong. Don't threaten. Don't think you've got the higher moral ground. Don't use the leverage or bargaining chip you may have over his head at the start. Just be a regular person without an attitude.

Organized labor is still paying the price for its arrogance in the days they had the market cornered. Some of you think and act like you still do. Like elephants, employers never forget and they are just looking for a reason to believe the worst about you. In summary, defy the negative stereotypes, inaccurate facts and outdated images.

For Nonbelievers: The Look

Am I getting through here? Still wearing your red, white and blue collar? Think I'm full of it? Let me convince you right now. Tell me when you last got "the look."

You know, you're at the barbecue or dinner party meeting. Someone you don't know asks you what you do for a living and you tell them you work for a union.

And then you get "the look."

Most every union leader in every audience I have ever spoken to has experienced "the look." What's up with that? You and I know very well what's up with that. You have been pre-judged in five seconds due to your affiliation with organized labor. That look is the obstacle that you, individually, and every member of your organization must overcome in your efforts to be recognized as a positive, ethical and forward-thinking partner in American business.

To you, the look is bullshit. But, the look is their reality.

- The look is stereotyping.
- The look is ignorance.
- The look is a belief system you must change.
- The look is waiting for you every day.
- There's nothing more to say.

CHAPTER 4

Your Clients: Rats, Scabs and Golden Geese

Love your enemies in case your friends turn out to be a bunch of bastards.

—R. A. DICKSON

The Employer Is Necessary

Like it or hate it, the concept is clear: the employer is necessary. He is, in fact, the most necessary component in the equation. You can have an employer, but no union. You cannot have a union without an employer. You need and depend on the employer. He is your Golden Goose so don't wring his neck or try reaching up his ass for "golden eggs" on demand. And because he is so necessary, don't resent him or punish him for it.

The Employer as Your Client

Since I deal with contractors, I can only use them as a prototype of the type of client you will be approaching. It is very important that you understand your client. An employer is, first and foremost, a businessman. His primary motivation must be the financial survival and success of his company. Therefore, he is most likely to be drawn to people who share his value system. Your client is likely to have most of the following characteristics:

- Competitive
- Confident
- Suspicious
- Problem Solver
- Analytical
- Aggressive

- Tough
- Risk Taker
- Strong Self-Image
- Highly Motivated
- Intense
- Focused

This type of individual is always looking to form alliances with people that understand, appreciate and tolerate his attitude and methodology. He is looking for alliances that offer value. He does not have time for people, organizations or vendors that do not add value to his pursuit of success. He is looking for problem solvers. He is looking for opportunity creators. He is looking for people he can count on and trust. He values long-term relationships and will be highly unlikely to enter into any business relationship unless it has long-term value. You need to be thinking about providing that value from day one.

Learn the Two Words

If I asked you to give me two words to describe a non-union employer, what would they be? Scab and Rat. I hear them shouted at me in all my seminars when I first ask the question. These are two words in your vocabulary that must change. There is a percentage of employers who may well be described as rats and scabs; exploitive and nasty characters. But there are many more who are not. Many more non-union employers deserve a new title. The correct two words are *Potential Client.*

These two words are a mind-set that you have to establish before you can ever be a successful organizer or marketer. The formula is pretty basic—if an employer is already union, then he is already your client. If he is non-union, then he is your *potential client*. You will never need to organize a unionized company because they are already a client. So, basically, all of your *potential clients* are non-union scabs and rats. The only future clients you will ever add will be non-union scabs and rats. The future of your union market share is with scabs and rats. Get it? I thought so. Get over the scab and rat stuff. Calling your potential client names makes no sense and is no way to do business. Frankly it appears to be "the look" except now you're the ones giving it.

Client Fears

Fear is the greatest obstacle to your effectiveness as a business development specialist. Your potential clients do not understand you and, in most instances, fear you.

They do not fear you individually. They fear you organizationally. They fear you as a threat to the viability of their business. They view you as a controlling entity. They see the union through a filter of inaccuracies, half-truths and bad histories. No matter what you say and do in your job, it is this fear that you must address.

This fear is quite understandable if you think about it. Don't we all fear new things? Don't we all fear changes that we are not in full control of? Don't we all evaluate people we don't know with a bit of healthy skepticism?

In most every organizing effort that I have been involved with, fear is the most universal condition of the potential client. As well, keep in mind how people act when they are afraid. Fight or flight?

Think of how you get over your fears. More information? One step at a time? Have someone you trust guide you? Total confrontation? Total rejection? Everyone has a pattern of how they deal with fears. Try to understand this and use it strategically. What is your potential client's greatest fear of doing business with you? What information or action can you engage him with to reduce or eliminate that fear?

Always remember—buying is an emotional decision and fear is probably the most powerful de-motivating emotional response there is.

Client Credibility Crash Course

What do you know about being a contractor or employer? Not too much, I would venture. So can you understand the operational, economic and competitive challenges of your client? I suggest a crash course to establish some credibility. The course outline for construction is roughly as follows:

1. Observe a client's bid being prepared.

Most union personnel have absolutely no idea how work is obtained. They have a vague idea that it is based on price and production and the contractor then makes millions of dollars. Watching a bid being prepared and analyzed is an educational essential. How can you serve a client if you don't understand how he procures work? I would suggest observing a job bid that is fairly large and complex and includes non-union competitors. Watch the contractor's and estimator's faces as it gets within ten minutes to bid opening. This is like watching NFL films in your own industry. Find a union contractor client and explain that you are accelerating the learning curve of your agents and organizers. Excellent beginning.

2. Read all client publications in your market.

With this little bit of homework, you will learn more about the market than you can imagine. Every area has bid reports for public and private work. Sometimes they are the Dodge Reports and, in other instances they are smaller publications. You will find the competitive story of your industry played out every day. I hear contractors bitch all the time about union personnel (including rank-and-file) who have no idea what is going on in the marketplace. Maybe it's just me, but it seems strange that many union leaders and organizers do not understand the potential of this basic information resource.

3. Arrange a client job shadow for all new agents and organizers.

Does this sound like high school? Job shadowing is a proven method of exhibiting specific aspects of a job, career or position. Pair up the new guy with a contractor, superintendent or project manager. They may see it as a nuisance, but persist. By asking them questions on their needs, problems, issues and concerns, you will begin to refine your own message in the field immediately. Do not wait. You'll never figure it out on your own. Besides, you'll have one guy in the industry who doesn't think you're a know-nothing idiot—he'll know it and like you anyway.

4. Learn the answers to the following questions:

- How much does re-work by your members cost the contractor each year?
- How does safety relate to workers compensation costs?

- After insurance, unemployment, disability and other mandatory contractor contributions, how much does a journeyman really cost per hour?
- What is the bidding margin of difference between your best/average employer and his top two non-union competitors?

In other industries there will be other lessons. Simply put, the more homework you do, the more credibility you will gain with your client.

CHAPTER 5

Targeting Potential Clients

A wise man knows everything, a shrewd one, everyone.
—ANONYMOUS

Create a Target Database

Hate the computer geeks? Me, too. Too damn smart and smarmy. But they've got "stuff." One powerful and essential tool they have that you need is a database or contact management software program. For those non-techies out there, a database is like a phone book you put together yourself—names, ranks, serial numbers, addresses, fax numbers and e-mails. This stuff is what marketing dreams are made of.

Every business has a list of clients. In today's world you don't keep them in a Rolodex, note card file or address book. You keep them in this basic database program. This "phone book" defines who is in your market, who the decision-makers are and how to reach them quickly and easily.

I recommend Microsoft Access or ACT as basic database/contact management programs. These are relatively easy to use. They track all contacts and responses. They provide decent reports and easy merges for purposes of letters, faxes, labels and e-mails.

Target Prioritization

When targeting, it's not a good idea to categorize anyone too quickly. Don't judge a book by its cover and all that stuff. However, it is important that you invest your time wisely in your business development process.

I would suggest that when you have more than five prospects you are working on, it is a good idea to prioritize your time investment. Try to figure, at a gut level, who is a yes or a maybe and invest your time accordingly. Don't be too quick to write someone off as a no. People and situations can change rapidly. You can really improve your results by simply staying in touch.

Targeting Little Guys

Decide now. Do you have the patience and foresight to water acorns? Can you help to grow mighty oaks? This is one strategy I advise for targeting prospective employers. Start with a company that is young, vital and aggressive. One that does not have a long history or operational tradition. One where the owner is not so insulated from the everyday operations that he cannot see the potential for change. One where existing profit-sharing programs do not need to be dismantled to allow for multi-employer benefit programs to be established. The idea is to approach it like a venture capital firm. Go after a large number of small companies with the idea that a certain percentage will make it big. And when they make it, if you have been cooperative and attentive to the needs of the client, you will share in the success and receive loyalty in return.

These companies, over time, will be a better investment of time and energy than chasing the really big boys who have the time, money and lawyers to keep you out.

Targeting Mid-Size Guys

Rapidly growing companies tend to need key personnel—especially in supervisory positions. Find them managers and leaders. It is vital for their continued growth in the business. If these individuals are already union members, it creates a strong incentive for employers to consider the merits of becoming unionized.

For these companies it is also important to perform the following research:

- What is the company's history?
- Where is he geographically operating?
- What is his estimated backlog?
- Who is the competition?
- What is the growth pattern?
- Who are the key decision makers?
- How does he treat his employees?
- What is his payment history?

All of these factors will become part of your "needs assessment" as you approach the employer. Better that you come prepared to show him that you know his business and needs up-front.

Knocking Down Dominoes

Everyone in the private sector watches their competition. It is a survival technique by which many companies "keep up with the Joneses." It is no different in the area of union organizing and business development. Your absolute best advertisement is a satisfied customer. This is defined as a newly signed company that can provide a testimonial that becoming unionized was, in fact, a good thing. They can testify that union reps are not boogey-men out to kill the profits and productivity of the company.

Do not underestimate the power of this synergistic exchange. Create a chart of your targeted employers. Figure out who knows who. Work along a linear pattern that logically connects those business leaders whose opinions and actions in the marketplace are likely to be closely examined and evaluated by others. Dominoes placed side by side or too far apart do not fall together. Use the relationships that exist to create your ongoing model for success.

Targeting Stinky Fish

I forget who said it, but the quote was "I wouldn't want to be a member of a club that would have me as a member." Sometimes having someone in the club or union, just to get another body is not really the best strategy. There are marginal employers that you may consider bringing into the union fold that act as "resource leeches." These employers are very high maintenance and require constant tending. Examples of their leeching might include ongoing trust fund problems, ongoing payment issues, personnel mistreatment...getting the picture? Now I know that some of this comes with the territory but who really wants a bad actor as a client? Does the financial benefit equate to the pain and woe that this employer is going to bring down on you? Before taking on a problem child, ask yourself, will this be my problem six months from now? Sometimes even a big fish is too stinky and ugly to land.

Seasons to Target and Solicit

There are specific times for approaching the client base for the construction industry. The best and worst of the seasons are illustrated below (10 as the best time and 1 as the worst):

Spring: Spring is a good time to approach an employer. He is preparing for an upcoming season and is looking over his arsenal to see if anything is missing. Also, this time of year is not too time intensive, although the employer is likely stressed-out due to perceived lack of work. About a 6.

Summer: Summer is a bad time to do real business development. Employers are in their busiest time of the season. They have little time for anything but the essentials. Sales and marketing appointments are for filling critical needs only. About a 4.

Fall: Fall is an excellent time to discuss options with any potential client. The season is almost over. Money has been made. Problems have been identified and addressed (or not, and that's where you come in). The workload is not so severe, and the employer is in a frame of mind to at least listen. Most of the marketing success that I have with my association is in the months of August, September, October and November. About a 7.

Winter: Winter is a mixed blessing. With all the rain, snow and downtime, people have time to talk. But winter is also a time of inaction. There is not a lot of urgency to the issues. Decisions can be put off until next season. This is a good time to work on relationships, not contracts. About a 5.

Sleeping With the Enemy

Most employers belong to associations of one sort or another. Many times unions look at these associations as "the enemy" because they represent the interests of the employers. I would suggest that this is a big mistake. Unions need to do more with, rather than against, employer associations. I know that many times in labor relations and legislative matters, the associations are actively working against your interests. However, it is possible to create other "away from the bargaining table" opportunities to work together on industry issues.

Over the past four decades, labor and management in our area did about 90 percent of our business and communicating at the bargaining table. We spent so much time cutting up the same pie, we stopped looking at how we might expand the pie for both parties. We eventually figured out that we had to start talking to each other away from the bargaining process.

After much discussion and planning, two unions representing almost 40,000 craft workers and three associations representing 1,700 employers, created a joint labor management organization, the California Alliance for Jobs. It was funded with $2 million of annual employer contributions. We now engage in aggressive business development programs and fight environmental restriction of the industry. We also lead state and local funding measures to benefit public works construction. Recently we jointly provided the leadership and resources to pass bond measures generating more than $25 billion worth of work in the state for union members and signatory contractors. As a founder and Secretary-Treasurer of this organization, I have seen and experienced the future.

The effort noted above is about expanding both market share and opportunity. It's about getting together with a different mind-set. The discussions around our table are strategic and optimistic. It is a sharing of ideas based on communication and cooperation. It is facilitated through the associations and unions and, as such, brings an entire industry together for the common good. It took a long time for us to create this cooperative model, but is has been well worth it.

Look at the associations in your area (even though right now many of you are thinking, "No way I'd ever work with *them*") and consider the possibilities. Associations are a direct line into the entire employer community. You can target all of the potential clients at one time. Rather than changing the perception of you and your union one employer at a time, you can have a much more significant and far-reaching impact if you are willing to try.

CHAPTER 6

Marketing 101

Tradition is what you resort to when you don't have the time or the money to do it right.
—KURT H. ADLER

Old School Marketing

Some union guys think that you don't need to change your marketing approach as time goes by. "Heck, we always did it that way, I just don't see why we have to change." Let's not change then. Let's say you are going down to Sears (or better yet, your local union hall) to buy a lawnmower. You get there and walk up to the salesman (old school labor representative) and your conversation goes like this:

"Hi. I'd like to buy a lawnmower."

"We've got the one you need."

"Great can you tell me the benefits?"

"F**k you. You're buying that one there."

"What do you mean?"

"I mean that you are going to buy this f**king mower right now and that's it."

"What if I don't?"

"We're coming over to your house and digging up your front lawn, you asshole. Then we are going to carry signs in front of your house that say you don't take good care of your lawn."

"Well, that is going to be pretty traumatic for my wife and kids."

"Not really. We went to your house and got the wife and kids to sign authorization cards that say you have to buy the mower."

Ah, the joys of the old school labor touch. The thing is, many old school agents and organizers couldn't sell free money by the bag-full in today's marketplace.

The guy needs the mower. He needs all the details and specifications. He needs to know about the horsepower, adjustments and free attachments. He needs to know about how it fits his lawn. He needs to learn about the right oil to gas mixture. He needs to know about the warranty. He has a million damn questions that go on and on and drive you crazy. And you'd do the same thing in his position. Modern marketing takes all of this into account.

Tailor your presentation to provide answers to the detail questions for they will come up over and over. Your product is much more complex than a lawnmower and, thus, you will need greater mastery of your marketing presentation content and format. Old school is out for good.

Marketing Instead of Negotiating

Think about the time you spend with employers. Many times you are in a negotiation-debate or conflict format. After a few years, you get used to it, and it can be hard to turn it off. You come to every discussion mentally trained to be in your negotiation-mode. Don't let yourself fall into that habit. It is vital that you see your role as an information provider and problem solver. You have so much to offer in terms of resources, expertise and opportunity. Don't mask it with your habitual negotiation game face.

Brand Names and Emotional Responses

When marketing a product or service, how important is the emotional connection between the customer and the product or service? Let's find out.

In column A, make a list of five brand names that you think are absolutely terrific. Products that you believe in. Products you would recommend. They can be any type of product or service brands. After you have completed column A, move across to the "Feeling After Purchase" lines and fill these in as well. How do you feel after you have purchased something you really believe in?

Column A:
Great Products / Services   Feeling After Purchase

_____   _____

_____   _____

_____   _____

_____   _____

_____   _____

Now, in Column B below, make a list of the brand names that you think are absolutely terrible. Brands you would never buy under any circumstances. Brands you would never recommend. List brands that you would not be caught dead using, buying or owning. Add the "Feeling After Purchase" segment associated with each of these products as well.

Column B:
Poor Products and Services   Feeling After Purchase

_____   _____

_____   _____

_____   _____

_____   _____

_____   _____

Now look at the lists and ask the following questions:
■ Why do you feel the way you do when you buy any of the products or services in Column A?
■ Why do you feel the way you do when you buy one of the products or services in Column B?

The point is that every brand creates a picture in the mind of the buyer. That picture in turn creates an emotional response. That emotional response is the key to the buying decision. Positive emotional responses include security, satisfaction, self-esteem, confidence and fulfillment. Negative emotional responses include fear, doubt, frustration, unhappiness and uncertainty.

Also, look at how your belief systems are represented in the Column B products and services. Many of these products you would not buy based on their policies, reputation or treatment of workers. Your decision is not simply an analysis of the item or service, but of the business philosophy of the company and how it compares to your own. The belief systems of many of your potential clients cast you in the same light.

This is what you need to keep in mind when you are marketing your product to both your existing union employers and to your potential clients. It is up to you, not them, to create positive images of your product and services. It is up to you to create the emotional ties to them that create loyalty and word-of-mouth endorsement. It is up to you to maintain the ethical and businesslike standards that will create the respect necessary for you to build long-term relationships. It is up to you to create the positive response.

Good Product
+ Strong Positive Image
+ Right Emotional Response

= **Decision to Purchase**

Marketing Materials

When you are looking to buy something where do you get the information? From advertisements, brochures, product guides or sales representatives. How does someone find out about being an employer with your union? How does one get their questions answered? Do you have a brochure? A video? A presentation packet? A question and answer sheet? Not likely. You probably have a collective bargaining agreement (that no one can understand anyway) and nothing else. How can you expect to use a collective bargaining agreement to sell anything? The real benefits must be explained. Common questions must be summarized and answered in writing. You need a professional piece and it's going to cost you.

One union I work with invested $25,000 on several thousand four-color brochures, with lots of photos and five inserts on various programs, services and benefits. This then became the opener for client relations. You may say that seems like an insane investment and the rank-and-file would go crazy if their dues money was spent like that? Well, I am pleased to report that this particular union signed 125 new companies in the year following that investment. Another union spent $2500 for 1500 simple but professional three-fold brochures. You've got to spend money to make money. Don't cheap out when it comes to creating high-quality presentation materials, and don't be sketchy in including all of the information that a prospective employer may find valuable.

Advertising

Very few products or services are so wonderful that they sell themselves without advertising. You are not that wonderful.

Of recent I have been impressed with the campaigns by the Laborers International, United Brotherhood of Carpenters and IBEW. I don't always agree with the marketing messages or campaign strategies, but they are at least putting out the good word. A consistent stream of good advertising can help turn around poor perceptions of products or services.

One example might be imported pick-up trucks. There was a time, not too long ago, when you would never see a Toyota or Nissan pick-up on the job site. Junky rattle trap vehicles? Not anymore. Toyota Tundra, Nissan Frontier and their knock-offs are everywhere. The ad campaigns helped make it alright to drive an import pick-up. Hey, if some print ads and TV time can get a red neck out of a Dodge and into an import, there's still hope for you.

Public Relations

Almost all press coverage of unions puts them in a terrible light. The only references you see relate to liberal politics, corruption, violence, or strikes. Labor needs a full public relations makeover in the eyes of American commerce and it begins at the local level.

Your unions are involved in many community-based programs—doing good things for people. This is a very important message to get out. It is your job to develop contacts with local newspaper editors, TV producers, cable access managers and similar. One contact can reach a million people with the right media placement. Get quoted on the business pages. Be the voice of the little guy. Be the down-home hard working volunteers. Be the community pillars. Be something besides the violent striker or shouting malcontent.

Astoundingly, in 1997, the most widely read engineering and construction magazine in the nation, *ENR* magazine, ran a very positive cover story on unions and the changes they are implementing. This article should be a promotional piece contained in every packet given to every prospective client that an agent or organizer approaches.

The power of public relations can be summed up as follows: if it's in print in a leading industry publication down to a local rag, most people will figure it is true and be influenced by it. Don't blame the media—use it.

Marketing Technologies

Three quick questions:

1. Do you have a web site where a non-union employer can anonymously get the complete list of benefits of union affiliation without anyone knowing or any obligation?

2. Do you have a sales or new employer orientation video covering the benefits of being union or your commitment to a business partnership? How about a CD? Did you know it only costs a buck to burn a CD?

3. Do you have a database of non-union employers for mailings, broadcast faxes or e-mails?

If you answered yes to all three of these, you understand the power of relatively inexpensive technology as marketing tools.

If you answered no to all three of these, I would suggest you form a small group of tech-savvy organizers or agents to formulate a strategy. Give them no money and no extra time at first. Tech-heads will do it just to do it. But when they show promise, establish a decent budget line item and give them credit for a job well done.

CHAPTER 7

The Marketing Message

Tell the truth and run.
—YUGOSLAVIAN PROVERB

Union Yes! Is Pure B.S.

Union Yes!

Union Yes what?

Spare me the American-made mom and apple pie routine. Unions don't have shit for market share and you give me "Union *yes!*" as the answer? How about "Hyundai *yes!*" " Arthur Anderson *yes!*" or "Martha Stewart *yes!*" Gutless slogans kill me.

Look, I know that message is for the rank-and-file. But what about the employer; the profit-minded bastard about to put thousands of union workers on his payroll? What does he want to read on the next ten million bumper stickers?

- Sell me some benefits.
- Sell me some value.
- Sell me something tangible and real.
- Sell me something I need.
- Sell me something to enhance my competitiveness.
- Sell me something to increase my profits.
- Sell me something I want.
- Sell me something we can partner on.
- Sell me on you.

You need to sell the employer community and marketplace twice as hard as the rank-and-file. You need your marketing message to get into the employer's eyes, ears and guts as well. "Union Yes!" might make everyone carrying a union card feel good but so does masturbation. Enough said.

Message Impacts and Imprints

See if you can fill in the blanks:

Marketing Slogan   *Company or Product*

Got _____?   _____

Like A Rock   _____

The Ultimate Driving Machine   _____

Have it Your Way   _____

Terry Bradshaw appears in ads for _____

Tastes Great, Less Filling   _____

America's Team   _____

Plop Plop, Fizz Fizz   _____

Not Your Father's   _____

Built Tough   _____

So what is the point? A consistent marketing message seeps into your brain and like it or not, you will retain it to a significant degree. Thus, carefully consider the message you want to place in the minds of both your existing and potential clients, and then pound it home again and again. Your message must focus on value, quality and return on investment.

CHAPTER 8

The Killer Sales Force

He had a God-given killer instinct.
—AL DAVIS

I'm Not a Salesman

Often I hear the scornful comment, "I'm not a salesman, I'm a union representative."

Welcome to the real world, Mr. Denial.

Do you sell yourself to your members to get elected or re-elected? Do you sell yourself to your boss? Did you sell yourself to your wife or husband before the "I do?" Don't play games with the artificial prestige of your self-image. Everyone sells. Honest people admit it.

Why is being a salesperson looked upon as something less than honorable? I say look at the product. I'm not talking about aluminum siding and used cars here.

Setting Sales Goals

No successful business in America operates without specific targeted goals and objectives for business development. Does your union have such goals? Do you? If not, why? A business development or organizing effort cannot measure success without goals.

I recall giving a presentation to a large group of union leaders and asking them how many new employers could be signed in a one-year period. I threw out the number 1,000—they laughed. Then I tried 500—they began to get serious. I then suggested 250—they began to look at each other. I finally tried 100 and many heads nodded. What's my point? There is a basic threshold of performance that all of the members of your business development team can understand and agree upon. It must be measurable and reasonably attainable based on the number of employers you are targeting in your market. It should challenge and motivate the team. Begin with the end in mind. Set a sales business development goal.

A Condition of Employment

It is my opinion that every single union representative working in the private sector should be responsible for organizing one company per year. No matter where I have given seminars, every union leader agrees that this is not an outrageous objective. To me, any representative that cannot create one new relationship in a year is in the wrong business. This minimal effort should be considered a condition of continuing employment.

Some might say "I can't do that." Ask those slackers if they knew they were going to be shot dead if they did not sign up a new company in 72 hours, could they do it? I'm sure most could. So really it comes down to the proper motivation. Let me be clear; I do not suggest shooting organizers or business agents. Most of the time.

Enthusiasm

"What I do best is share my enthusiasm."
—BILL GATES, MICROSOFT CORPORATION

That's how he became the world's richest man. Not by doing it all himself, but by getting others to share in his enthusiasm. Enthusiasm is contagious. It is motivating. It soothes the tired and revitalizes the discouraged. It is an intangible that anyone can see and feel when in someone's presence that has it. It is another condition of employment in this business. It is the secret weapon.

Perseverance

Accept the fact right now that it is going to take you multiple visits, presentations and contacts to bring in a prospective employer. Why? Because you need to establish a relationship. Would you get married to someone after the first date? Of course not. It takes a period of time for the employer to understand who you are and how your union conducts business. It takes time to digest the materials you have submitted to him for consideration and answer his questions. You cannot be discouraged by the fact that you have to try and try again. Expect that it will take five times, at least, and possibly twice that number. Now you say, "Wow! That sure seems like a waste of time just to get one employer." Try looking at the big picture and really analyzing the value of a new client.

Rejection

Let's look at one of the biggest obstacles to successful organizing and business development efforts—fear of rejection. No one likes to be rejected. No one likes to take a hit on his ego. When people say no, we often take it personally. We often become hostile to the person rejecting us. We sometimes lose heart.

Are you willing to put yourself out there on the edge of your ego and take a punch? Are you willing to come back with a smile after being kicked in the teeth? Can you separate your professional objectives from your personal identity? Think about it.

A Reject's Motivation

As previously noted, sometimes it can be very difficult to develop any meaningful traction. Rejection weighs heavy on you. About the time you start feeling like a loser, I'd suggest you remember the following quote:

> "I got cut from the varsity basketball team as a sophomore in high school. I learned something. I knew I never wanted to feel that bad again. I never wanted to have that taste in my mouth, that hole in my stomach. Ever."
> —MICHAEL JORDAN, NBA'S GREATEST PLAYER

What "F**k You" Really Means

"F**k you" does not mean no. It means, "I don't have enough information on your product or service." It means, "Your timing is bad." It means, "I don't yet see the merits of your product or service." It means, "Try again later." It means, "I've been burned before and now I'm shy." It means, "What are you really made of?" It means, "Give me some time to think this over." It means, "I don't know you well enough to trust you yet." No does not mean no. When you hear a F**k You or a no, it is time for you to re-evaluate your approach, refine your materials and try again.

Stay Hot

When you are working on a hot prospect, you need to stay on them and work them. Do not let time go by (defined as more than one week) because you are too busy, too preoccupied with other prospects, or getting lazy.

If you let the trail get cold, you will never make up for the lost time.

Exploit the Trend

In the next 5 to 10 years it is projected that there will be a major shortage of workers for the construction industry, high-tech manufacturing and many other hands-on fields. Thus, the trend now is one where supply and demand may be swinging back towards workers as a valued commodity. Thus, unions should be doing everything possible to compete with other professions to reach and recruit the next generation of workers for our industry. Apprenticeship programs are fine, but far too few really talented and aggressive individuals are going to be willing to put up with four to five years to reach the fiscal rewards of their prospective profession.

I agree this is unfortunate, but it is also a trend. The immediate gratification mode is upon us. Work as our life identity is not what it was. The best and the brightest have incredible opportunities these days. The challenge is to get out in front of the trend. To find and train these individuals is labor and management's critical challenge. Remember that all you really have to sell is the competitive capacity of your workforce. As they age and are (or are not) replaced by skilled individuals, our competitive ability in the market will either thrive or die.

Celebrate the Win

When you win, celebrate. Ever watch the end of a hotly contested NFL, NBA or MLB playoff game? See the players give each other the hugs and high-fives? The big grins? The intense satisfaction of winning? The total feeling that nothing can stop them? For that moment, they are kings.

I am big on offshore sport fishing—marlin, sailfish, dorado. But I got the fever on my first fish, a marlin off of Maui. Not too big, about 100 pounds. But on a 30 pound test line and light tackle, the reel screamed. The fish danced on the water time after time. And 45 minutes later, I reeled that bastard in and right at the boat, it came off the hook. It lay there stunned and the mate rammed the gaff into it—then he slipped and smacked his balls right on a fish box. The marlin was pulled aboard, wildly swinging its lethal snout, the mate groaning on the deck. I was stuck, buckled to the fighting chair—trying to avoid getting my legs cut off. By the end of that fight I felt pretty jacked up. Like, "C'mon, let's do it again. Right now!" And that gave me the fever for a lifetime. I can spend a lot of down time working my ass off waiting for that feeling again.

When you succeed, take a moment to savor it. Do not cheat yourself or your team out of the true fulfillment and winning feelings that come with the kill.

Star Players

In each organization, there are star players hiding. These are individuals who possess the combination of mental toughness, exceptional communication skills, powers-of-persuasion, sense of humor, aggressive attitude and self-motivation. When you identify these individuals, nurture their talents. It may require reassignments of responsibilities. It may require a change in territories. It may require dealing with political obstacles. It may require a significant investment in his personal or professional development. My advice? Whatever it takes—do it.

These rare individuals are the "rainmakers" for organized labor. They usually comprise less than five percent of all labor representatives. You'll know them when you see them. So give them the resources to make it happen and then stand back.

Structured Strategy Sessions

I strongly suggest that the union hold highly structured monthly meetings with those involved in business development. These meetings should be structured to maximize performance and accountability. The agenda should be limited to:

■ Prospect calls—who was called? When? What is the follow up?

■ Obstacles, issues and problems each person is dealing with. Request for advice from the group.

■ New strategies, information, books, literature, articles, industry trend reports.

- Who will be called in the upcoming week or month?
- Recognition for results and top performers

These are just a few suggestions on the content of these meetings. Whatever you cover is not as important as making sure that you keep them up on a consistent basis. Consistency in keeping some form of organized effort in the spotlight, over a long period of time, is the key to success in any marketing and sales venture.

Sales Training

If unions invest anything in their front-line organizers and business development specialists, they should consider professional sales training. This can be as generic as Dale Carnegie courses, to community college courses on sales and marketing, to one-day seminars on specific techniques. This type of information can be learned in the field, but you will lose many potential clients along the way. The fastest and most effective method I endorse is putting someone through several courses and then letting them experiment with it in the field. Professional training is just a smart way of acknowledging the obvious—you don't go to a gunfight with a knife...you have to have the right weapons or tools for the job.

CHAPTER 9

Proven Tactics and Strategies

One must change tactics every ten years if one wishes to maintain superiority.

—NAPOLEON BONAPARTE

10,000 Calls in Five Minutes

This is a simple and killer formula for an extensive marketing outreach effort that will cost you absolutely nothing. It will take five minutes per week to implement. You will reach thousands of existing clients and potential clients—boost visibility for your organization, exceed expectations and defy stereotypes...it's all waiting for you to implement the following directive.

Everyone in your organization must make two phone calls per week to contact one existing union client and one prospective non-union client.

Let's talk about the impact of this simple formula.

If ten agents and organizers make two calls per week, there will be 1,040 calls and contacts made over a one-year period.

If fifty agents and organizers make the calls, there will be 5,200 calls and contacts made in one year.

If one hundred agents and organizers make the calls, there will be 10,400 calls made. You get the picture.

Questions for doubters:

- Who does not have time to make two phone calls per week?
- What positive impact will there be as a result?
- What is the downside?
- What excellent habits does this form for the agents and organizers?
- What is the compound impact of this over months and years?

- When was the last time anyone called an existing union employer just to check in on what he might need?
- What do you think your existing employer will think the first time you call? How will his thinking change after he gets three or five or ten of these "check-in" calls?
- What will the impact of thousands of phone calls to non-union potential clients be?

Five minutes. No added costs. Thousands of contacts. Awesome upside potential. Make the calls.

Favors, Chits and Contacts

Sometimes it takes a little favor or chit from someone to get a door opened. This is the time for you to call in favors in return for those you have performed for your existing union employers. Every union rep I have ever known has had to exercise flexibility and sometimes arbitrary judgment that directly or indirectly favors an employer. This can be as subtle as a turned head up to direct intervention in a difficult or messy matter. If you're in the business, you know what I mean. These favors are not without value. They can be traded for small considerations that can open doors for you that might otherwise be closed. Do keep in mind that this should not be approached as a "you owe me" type of exchange—more in the spirit of professionals exchanging favors and resources that are mutually beneficial. And when someone comes through for you, don't forget a thank you note.

Internal Resources

Sometimes it is virtually impossible to get an appointment with the principal of a company. Here is where your knowledge of the internal structure of a company can work best. I make it a point to know the names of every secretary and assistant of most every influential person I deal with. Further, I try to make it a point to be the most pleasant person she will deal with in the course of her business day.

Beyond this, you should know who runs operations, finance, human resources or any other key departments that may be consulted in the process of evaluating your proposals. Any or all of these people may be the entry point for you to begin a relationship with the company.

Gatekeepers

How often must we all deal with the "gatekeepers?" Almost daily. These are people entrusted with the following tasks:

- Preventing anyone from wasting the boss's time
- Forestalling salespeople from presenting information to the wrong people
- Lying about the boss being in a meeting because he never wants to talk to the calling party
- Juggling fifty things a minute
- Doing a great job and generally being under-appreciated for it

Understanding this dynamic makes all the difference. First, you should know the names of the secretaries and executive assistants in the offices of your existing and potential clients. You cannot imagine the power that knowing someone's name creates for you (the positive image and the basic emotional connection). Also greeting or thanking the person by name is both courteous and classy.

And even if it is the gatekeeper's role to tell you he is not in for the fortieth time, you thank her and let her know your interest in talking to the boss. Eventually, you'll have her telling him that you deserve a chance and likely as not, she'll become a subtle advocate. Remember, for someone who does not get a lot of "strokes," these people perform a very vital function. They have a great degree of latitude to decide who gets put through to the boss.

Setting Appointments

Make yourself spend a specific amount of time each week setting appointments with employers. A basic suggestion would be to make five attempts per week. This can be combined with your two calls per week or (preferably) added to it. This must be done religiously. As in "if I don't make these calls, my hair will all fall out," or "my Viagra won't work." Get it? You are working on the laws of numbers here. Two calls a week is 104 calls a year. Five calls are 260. To begin with you might only get a one in ten to twenty hit ratio, if you are lucky. In summary, I can absolutely guarantee results—if you don't call, you will get no results. If you do call, you will get results.

Getting Appointments

The art of making an appointment might be the difference between success and failure. Some rules of thumb might include:

■ Find someone he knows to use as an introduction: "So-and-so suggested I give you a call."

■ Ask for a limited amount of time. "I'd like just 20 minutes of your time to introduce myself."

■ Stick to it. Remind him that you only asked for the 20 minutes and let him invite you to stay longer.

■ Be specific as to time and place. "I'd like to come by on Wednesday at 8 A.M., if that would be alright." Note: do not try for Mondays or any late afternoon appointments. In my opinion, the best time for appointments are early mornings at their office—the earlier, the better. This way there are no distractions, you are not competing with other crises and it's hard to be hostile early in the morning.

Anatomy of an Appointment

Here are just a few mandatory basics that you should cover in the meeting when you are successful in obtaining an appointment:

- A self-introduction and background to establish credibility.
- State the reason you are there to provide focus.
- Ask about the history of the company to get an overview of the company position.
- Ask about the individual's industry experience—it breaks the ice and everyone loves to talk about themselves.
- Tell him about your product in a brief, positive and enthusiastic manner.
- Follow-up on materials. They have likely been sent in advance, so you want to address questions and concerns.
- Provide references, testimonials or contacts to reassure prospects.
- Spend 70 percent of the time talking about him, 5 percent about you and 25 percent about your product.

If you can accomplish most of this in your first meeting, you will have done well. If you find yourself drifting, get back to the basics. Be sensitive to time issues and don't overstay your welcome.

It's a Conversation

No one I know likes to be sold anything. Most people (including me) will tell a salesperson that they don't need help even when they do. Why? Because they don't want to be sold. Ever been at an auto dealership (or better yet in the office of the so-called high-pressure closer) and you feel the squeeze before it even comes? Potential clients need all the essential components of your product or service communicated to them but in a conversational fashion. Don't push the sale too hard or too early. As you conduct your client meetings, consider yourself an educator first and a salesperson second.

Ask Vital Questions

In any business situation, no one is going to give you all the information that you need to execute a good game plan. Questions that are carefully crafted to obtain important information should be considered before you ever step into an office.

One time, when I visited a powerful labor leader, I was met by two very large guys in the parking lot who knew my name. They led me through three sets of locked doors (including his office door) and plunked me down in the middle of an office that looked like a tornado had hit five minutes before. I had a lot of questions about that unusual situation as it obviously had the potential to impact me in a dramatic way.

Carefully, and without him really even noticing, I asked a series of very basic questions about his local union and life. More than 10 questions in a row—and he loved every minute of it. Why? Because he was talking about his favorite subjects—his interests, his family, his local, himself. Everyone loves to talk about things and people that interest them. Are you and I any different?

We could have gone on forever but, after 10 questions, I had a good idea of who he was, where he came from, what he was thinking, how powerful he was, where his weaknesses were, why all the doors were locked and what I was expected to say and do in order to get what I needed. I never pitched or flattered or "third-degreed" him. Just a series of friendly questions leading to more friendly questions leading to answers and conclusions.

Ask questions. Listen. Analyze. Formulate. Act.

Address Objections First

You *must* sell against the client objections first. No amount of tact, persuasion or suede-shoe showmanship will eclipse the mind-set that pre-exists your arrival. Again, we are talking about making emotional inroads here. It is often through acknowledging known problems and concerns that you gain credibility. It is through addressing your primary negative images that you open the door. He cannot and will not hear anything else until you show him you understand his fear and reluctance.

Until you can talk to him straight, he hears you selling him used cars and Thigh Masters.

Polite Debating

Now, you might find this assignment difficult, but I am asking you to go out into the world to find people who probably completely disagree with your life's mission, goals and politics. Then I am asking you to begin a dialogue with these people who, under normal social conditions, you might want to punch, kick or at the very least spit on.

It's not quite that bad, but it is important to understand that you may not have too much in common right off the bat. It is further important to remember this simple concept going in, or you may react emotionally to what you perceive as an attack on the way you think or feel.

Polite debating is the fine art of pointing out or presenting information the other party might not readily agree with, but will not immediately reject. Kind of like planting the seeds of possibility in the other party's mind. If you are facing an individual who wants to convince you that your position is wrong, you can make one of two choices: engage them in an argument, or listen carefully and politely and then provide qualified comments such as "Well, I understand you feel strongly about that, but do you think at least the possibility exists that the earth might be round?" It is important to allow the other party the choice of considering the possibility that something might be true, of value or beneficial. You should never think that it is up to you to convince anyone of anything, ever. There is only one person who can convince anyone of anything—one guess.

Wish Lists:
From "No" to "What If..."

This is how you go from "no" to "what if." Ask him this question: "If I could do anything for you—if there were no limitations in any way, shape or form, what would it take for you to do business with our union?"

This is an effort to get out of the rut of looking at what you have and what he does not want. This is a way to get a dialogue going that opens up worlds of possibilities. He may not have any idea you can do a number of things for him. You both may learn that the obstacles are not as numerous or complex as you once thought.

Beyond this, it is always good to know which issues are the biggest obstacles to your organizing efforts. After you hear specifics from the client you'll find that many political and economic obstacles usually exist. Addressing these can be tough, especially with union old-timers and some rank-and-file. This may be one area where you need to make an assessment of whether the political heat is worth the additional market share.

Most importantly though, if you can get to wish lists, you are closer to the point of sale. You are no longer talking about the yes or no of doing business with the employer, but have moved on to discussing terms. Even though his wish list may not be as realistic as you would like (or in any way resembling your contract), you still have the opportunity for a give and take discussion.

Be a Problem Solver

Everyone loves a problem solver. Businessmen really love them because most of them spend 75 percent of their time "fire-fighting" unanticipated issues, challenges and skirmishes. If you can be a problem solver for a prospective client, you are already halfway home. When you do your homework on the company you are soliciting, find out what challenges they are facing—seeking key personnel, political problems with city hall, looking for training resources, etc. It is very helpful if you can walk in the door and show how you and your union can work to assist in providing solutions.

While you are at it, you might concentrate some of this problem solving capacity on your existing union clients. When you call them now *you are* the problem. Maybe you could get them to see you in a different light if you brought them solutions rather than problems.

Be Prepared to Close the Sale

Always have a contract with the accompanying paperwork available when you meet with an employer. From personal experience, I know when someone has made the emotional shift necessary to make the decision, you had better be ready to capitalize. If you have to get back to him or send him something, odds are you will lose 75 or more percent of those sales opportunities. Always be prepared to close the sale…on his cue.

Effective Closing Lines

Although it may seem distasteful, it is important to know how to wrap up a deal. You can't expect the client to do it for you. Here are several effective closing lines that allow you to request the business in a realistic and respectable manner.

- So, are you willing to try this out to see how it will work for you?
- Have I addressed all of your concerns?
- What will it take to get us started?
- I'm not asking you to sign your life away. Just to give it a try.
- Let me prove to you that this is a good thing for your business.

If these don't ring true for you, then develop some of your own. Remember, it is up to you to bring about closure. Don't just stand there with your big fat pen in your hand.

FAQs for Employers

This is the number one tool I suggest you prepare for your business development campaigns—Frequently Asked Questions. You need to put together a written question and answer sheet of all of the possible questions an employer could have about becoming unionized.

One union I worked with developed over sixty questions with detailed answers to each one. Why is this so important? Let us count the ways:

- Provides a uniform training guide for every business agent and organizer.
- Everyone has the same answer to the hard questions.
- Even a poorly trained representative can still drop these off to a potential client
- Written explanations have greater credibility
- Written answers have a much longer life than something verbal
- They can be used in discussions, in letters, on faxes, in brochures, on web sites, in advertisements or any other medium that you may utilize

What kinds of questions are we talking about? Try these for some examples:

- Is the union going to control my business?
- Is it true I can never fire anyone?
- Will the union allow me to use my existing workforce?

- How do the trust funds work? How are the benefits paid?
- Are there different (more competitive) rates of pay for new employees?
- How does the subcontracting provision work?
- Am I going to be less competitive as a union contractor?
- How long does the contract last? Is it permanent or can I get out if I don't like it?
- What are my guys going to have to pay to be members and what benefits do they get?
- Are the BAs going to pressure me to use unskilled hands?

Look at these as just the tip of the iceberg. Hold a quick brainstorming session and have someone put up all the questions on a flip chart and then select the most relevant. Don't overwhelm a prospect with all of them at once. A great tactic is to fax your prospects five to ten per week for six to eight weeks along with the same list of all of your benefits each time.

FAQs for Employees

It is estimated that the average person only retains about 10 percent of what they hear each day after they hear it, and even less after that. Thus, you can talk until you are blue in the face and the employees you are trying to educate or inform are unlikely to understand or appreciate the entire range of opportunities you are putting in front of them. On top of that, how can you expect them to explain the details to a spouse or co-worker at a later date?

Thus, you need to develop the FAQ sheet for employees.

The most frequently asked questions, for which you will need to develop uniform and persuasive answers, will generally be:

- What does the union get out of this?
- Will my wages go up or down?
- How much are my union dues going to cost?
- What do you use union dues for?
- What do I get out of this?
- What is the health coverage?
- I don't care about pensions in 20 years, I want my cash now. Why should I even care about retirement?
- Is this going to hurt my relationship with my boss?
- Is the boss going to fire me or replace me sometime down the road?
- What are the important rules in the contract that I should know about?

I'm sure that the bottom-up organizing training programs do an excellent job at outlining these questions for workers, so these are just the preliminary questions provided as an example. You may have to deal with know-it-alls, devil's advocates and all kinds of other pain-in-the-ass types that will make the process difficult. I would suggest that you combine a group meeting with individual meetings because many people are too shy to bring up their concerns in a group and will need a little hand holding along the way.

Employee Concerns

Sometimes you will have to deal with objections and complications that will extend beyond the owners or principals of the company. The hidden obstacle will be the impact on existing employees. The grass-roots skills you have acquired from working with your members should be of great assistance.

The major obstacles that you will need to explain or market the value of might include:

- Reduction in take-home wage to support a significant increase in fringe benefits
- Vacation pay policies and disbursements
- Pre-existing profit sharing or 401(k) plans
- Union dues (including supplementals or other hidden costs)
- Hiring hall rules
- Restrictions on mobility
- Health benefits and hours banking

Many deals have gone sour because the business development specialists took for granted the employees of the company would figure being union was a great deal. Remember that you are a late arrival. The company and the employee have a pre-existing relationship based on economics and employment history. Do not be arrogant in your assumption that you have "The Answer." Assume they both will be suspicious in adding you as the third wheel, and that you will need to be extremely well prepared and informed in your presentations.

You anticipate these issues and cover them in your FAQ sheets. Much of this information is likely available (although in a complex format) from your trust funds.

Saying Goodbye

After you are through presenting, threatening or groveling, depending on your style, it's time for goodbye. Think this is insignificant? Not quite. The closure of the meeting is the final tone. That tone should be sincere and appreciative even if the client was an arrogant jerk. He could be testing. He could still have his defenses up. He could still be dealing with the old union stereotypes but still like you. Be polite and thank him sincerely, but also let him know that you will look forward to:

■ Working with him in the future.

■ Discussing the opportunity further.

■ Sending him more information.

Goodbye is not "see ya." It is the temporary hold on your relationship until next time. Leave him feeling good about *you* even if he hates your union.

Thank You Notes

Never underestimate the power of a thank you note. In business, people are getting ruder and less considerate all the time. By sending a thank you note to someone that has taken time to see you, consider your proposal, or simply reject you and throw your ass out, you are showing you are one of the rare types who have basic manners—someone who cares. I suggest the local union print up thank you notes for all agents and representatives. Keep these in your desk drawer with envelopes and stamps (so it's not some major effort to send one).

I send about two thank you notes a week to people who have done me favors or who deserve a note of appreciation. It may not sound like much but, even at that rate, I am able to remind 100 business contacts each year that I care. Over the 18 years I have been in this business, it starts to add up.

Negotiating the Contract

At some point in time you have to negotiate a contract. Bottom-up or top-down—that day will come. If it is easy, then it will be a matter of discussing and perhaps arguing over terms and conditions. If it is bad, it will be a personal war between adversaries and their attorneys—threats, claims, counter-claims, NLRB charges and worse.

It has been said, when approaching a task, keep the end in mind. More simply put, the company is not organized until you get the contract. If you persist in a bottom-up campaign and end up with the employer at the bargaining table, you want to have a foundation established where communication is possible.

Although this seems unlikely since you have just jammed an election up his ass, it is still up to you to maintain a professional, cordial and "customer service" mode of communication for contract negotiations.

Look at this not as a concession to the employer but as an investment in a rapid resolution to contract negotiation. Contract negotiations can be a very time intensive effort that bears little fruit. Attempt to develop an underlying foundation of communication, no matter how bad it appears on the surface. Besides, the day this employer signs that agreement, he becomes your ally, your customer and your golden goose. Why wait for the signature to start treating him that way?

Organizing Agreements

This may be a new concept, but it is still a vital one. Everyone wants something extra. Every employer wants a little perk, consideration or advantage. It is the nature of the beast. You need to have something extra to give him besides a contract and a promise.

An organizing agreement is an up-front memorandum of understanding or contract addendum that provides specific terms and conditions by which the employer will become signatory to a contract. It contains little tweaks, reassurances and commitments that meet with the needs or concerns of the potential client. I have authored over 100 of these agreements and they basically look the same.

Note: Most organizing agreements I have been involved with were drafted by the employer and union together—not by an attorney. The more lawyerly you get, the less likely you will have a good outcome. This is not to say that a lawyer should not review the agreement if there are provisions that could become legal problems for the union. But, for the most part, attorneys are not paid to walk the gray line with you and will give you every conceivable reason not to do something. Use your best judgment but don't be irresponsible by promising more than you can legally deliver.

Next is content. Most organizing agreements have some basic components. These are outlined as follows:

- **Duration:** The organizing agreement should extend between 6 to 12 months, beginning with the date the memorandum is signed.

- **Existing Work Exemptions:** If a company has existing work with fixed costs that do not include union scale, benefits or rules, then specific projects are noted and exempted. Sometimes all private work is exempted or treated in a different manner.

- **Instant Health and Welfare Coverage:** A non-union contractor may have existing employees under a health plan. Most union agreements require a certain amount of hours to be worked prior to health coverage eligibility. This requires the employer to double-pay premiums. Eliminate this extra cost and you have removed one more economic barrier.

- **Mobility:** To the maximum degree allowed by your contract, give all existing employees full and immediate mobility within the area covered by the agreement.

- **Flexibility:** This usually covers being able to hire a specific number of people over a specific time period outside of the hiring hall regulations. This includes finding, interviewing and hiring. Flexibility may also extend to certain work rules or other issues pertaining to the specific nature of work. This is a delicate issue if your contracts contain a "favored nations" clause; however, creative language generally can overcome these obstacles. (I might suggest the existing union employers who would be invoking the favored nations clauses make an exception for a short-duration organizing agreement as it serves their long-term economic interests.)

- **Conflict Resolution:** This is a mutual promise that the employer will not suffer any job action prior to the parties being able to resolve the issues. Generally, giving them 48 hours to straighten something out is pretty reasonable.

- **Reduced Initiation Fees for Employees:** This can apply both to existing or prospective employees. Usually I suggest it be reduced by at least 50 percent.

- **Specialized Training Programs:** If the union has a good training program for apprentices and journeymen, I suggest that any special programs (Safety, First Aid/CPR, etc.) be offered to the company at no or low cost.

- **Treatment of Other Business Interests or Dual Shops:** This gets a little sticky, but sometimes the employer has similar, but not identical, business interests that could become contractually bound. Does it have to be all or nothing for the union? This can be a silent objection or a future problem if not addressed right from the start of the relationship.

Communicating Progress

Ever see the little red thermometer that community organizations post to show how much money has been raised for the Red Cross, the church roof or other noteworthy causes? These people understand the power of communicating results.

If you have set a business development goal, it is vitally important that the union find a method to communicate the progress (or lack thereof) towards that goal. Some methods that I suggest are large poster boards, plaques or charts in bright colors posted at the local union. With this communication comes accountability for results—a key motivator. Basically, if you are doing a great job—or a terrible job and no one knows—what's the difference?

CHAPTER 10

Your Professional Performance

Diamonds are only lumps of coal
that stuck to their jobs.
—B. C. FORBES

Appearance

Why is it that many labor reps believe they are exempt from basic grooming and attire standards? Why do I want to do business with a guy who looks unprofessional or unconcerned with appearance? As an employer, everyone in the business world who is seeking to establish my confidence and relationship—be they attorney, accountant, insurance agent, vendor or material supplier—looks better than you. Sorry to say, but the contrast does you no favors. Psychologists estimate that most people make up their minds about someone in less than one initial minute (and even less if they have a preconceived notion about you). Make the effort. Look good. Not slick, just somewhere between casual-dressy and professional. Do not wear your union jacket to employer meetings.

Eye Contact

Do not underestimate eye contact as a method of communication. An honest man looks me in the eye. A man I can count on does not avert his eyes when I ask a tough question. They say that the eyes are the windows to the soul. When I evaluate a prospective business partner of any sort, the look in his eyes will tell me more than he thinks it will.

Practice keeping your focus and maintaining steady eye contact.

Handshakes and Greetings

Do not work out your macho insecurity with the vise-grip handshake. Play little power games with your own peers or staff but not your clients. Give a good strong shake and hold it for a second. Look him in the eye and say either:

- Thank you for meeting with me today, *His Name*.
- It's a pleasure to meet you, *His Name*.
- Key item as noted above: *His Name*.

Active Listening

This is the most valuable skill you can develop as a business development specialist. You've got to listen to hear the potential client tell you what he needs. You've got to listen for him to tell you what he likes or dislikes. You've got to listen to the tone of his voice to read his intentions, apprehensions or fears. The old saying still holds, "better to keep your mouth shut and be thought a fool, than to open it and remove all doubt."

Body Language

There have been enough books written on these subjects by real experts, but let me just review the essentials:

- **Eye Contact:** As noted, do not deviate from direct eye contact. Do not let your attention wander. Stay focused on the person with whom you are talking like the next word they say could cure cancer.

- **Handshake:** Be sincere in a greeting and use the person's name. Even if you have just been introduced, make sure you restate it to them: "Very nice to meet you John/Sally."

- **No Crossed Arms:** This is an instinctive reaction to hostility. Do not show negative feelings. If you go into the defensive posture, your mind-set will quickly follow.

- **Seating Arrangements:** In most discussions of any gravity, the parties will put themselves across from each other. A table or desk can be the first of many obstacles in the discussion. If possible try to find alternatives to face-off seating arrangements.

- **Voice Intonation:** Be positive and businesslike. Do not assume you are pals in any informal manner. I spend most of my life on the phone, as do many business people. I can tell from even the most subtle voice inflections if the person I am dealing with is happy, pissed, bored, distracted, tired or defensive. In many instances I can tell if they are telling the truth or lying.

Listening to yourself is virtually impossible. But if you could listen to yourself for a day, you would be amazed at the information you give by the tone, pattern and inflection of your voice. Be aware of it in all business and negotiation situations. It tells a tale to others that you cannot hear yourself.

Control Your Emotions

Ever see a NFL team lose a big game because some wild-eyed linebacker went crazy? Emotional overload causes many problems in the business world. Leave your ego, attitude and pride in your heart of hearts. If you don't, eventually someone is going to provoke you into an "unsportsman-like conduct" foul. Afterwards, when you've lost the game, you'll be wishing you could have that one over again (even though, in your opinion, the guy really was an asshole and did deserve it).

Don't Let it Get Personal

The title speaks for itself. Oftentimes the problem with business is that it is a competition. There is a winner and a loser. The problem with many people is that they are very poor losers. Here is the only thing you need to remember. It's all business. When you win, it's business. When you lose, it's business. Never make someone lose face when you win. Try not to take a personal grudge away from a deal when you lose. This is easier said than done, but the price can be high. I know from experience. Allow me to share a true story.

So, this business agent wants a sit-down with me over a non-union company working in his jurisdiction. I tell him I can get the guy signed, let's sit down for breakfast. We do. He says this is the way it's going to be. I say that with a few other items, we can do it. He says, no, you don't understand, it's my way or the highway and walks out without paying for his coffee. Okay, he's posturing, nothing personal. Next day on the job are the pickets and the signs. My name, the contractor's name, vandalism and the media. Okay, we can do business without this guy for now. The company signs with four other unions—no problems, everyone loves us. Now this guy makes it his life. He sues. He goes to the television stations. He tries to pull audits. He calls the state and OSHA and everyone else. Okay, we say, enough. F**k this guy and the horse he rode in on. He's making it personal. So, he gets nothing. Ever. And so, eight years later he still has no contract with the company, other unions do his work—and it's probably never going to change.

After all is said and done, I have maybe three people in this business that I simply do not like at all. I don't like or trust them since they have done things to me in a pre-meditated and sometimes malicious manner. If they look at me sideways I will f**k them. They've earned being treated that way and they'll probably do the same to me if given the opportunity. That's not too bad for twenty years on the front lines of labor relations. But that's the problem with making business personal; it doesn't go away. It festers and fidgets and just waits for an opportunity to pop back up. It leaves bad feelings and nasty intent. It's just not worth it. When you get confused as to what is business and what is personal, you better take a long look at yourself and ask if you don't have a little too much ego invested in the job. Because it's either ego or sheer stupidity that makes people forget—it's just business.

Don't Gossip or Badmouth

If everything that was ever said about you reached your ears, you'd have no friends. Understand? Almost everybody talks smack about everyone else at one time or another. So remember, no matter who you are talking to, you have to expect that they are going to tell someone else what you've said. So why is this a big deal? Because if you talk about people or badmouth people, it will get back to them. If they are existing clients, other union leaders, potential clients, it doesn't matter, your need to trash talk does not exceed the value of your restraint.

In my office, you gossip or badmouth anyone around me one time only. If it hurts someone, next time you can brush up the resume. No one needs that kind of negativity in their operation, and it's usually a small number of people who do it out of their own insecurity. Say something nice about people and it gets back to them, too. Think about it. What are people saying about you right now?

Make 'Em Laugh

Think of a person in your life that makes you laugh a lot. I would bet a hundred bucks that you like that person. It is no coincidence. According to many surveys, sense of humor is ranked by women as one of the most attractive traits of a man. Moral of the story? It is a very powerful tool in creating a magnetic connection between people. I'm not suggesting that you try to date your clients—I am suggesting that you use humor wherever possible to break the ice, open a dialogue or ice the deal.

One time in a deadly serious negotiation, there were nearly 30 people on both sides of the table. We had been at it for seven months. The union leader had cussed us out real good all morning. So after lunch when he started in with "you're trying to f**k us over" and "stop putting a bunch of bullshit in front of us," we stopped the negotiation and responded, "Tom, since 8 A.M. this morning we have a count of 25 f**ks, 11 shits and 14 damns. We've got to even it up." And with that the 30 of us on our side of the table all counted 1-2-3 and yelled, "F**K YOU!" After the shocked look on their faces wore off, we all laughed for about five minutes. The entire negotiation changed after that. We settled two days later. I have seen some of the most masterful negotiators use humor at the right time and completely change an outcome. Why not you?

Taking life too seriously is a big problem for many of us. Employers have this problem to a greater degree than most people do. Thus, it is very important that you do not become just one more person who wants something from them with a grim look on your face and desperation in your eye.

Learn a few good jokes. Poke fun at your own expense (or if you want real good reviews, at your own union's expense) and you will find that barriers and defense mechanisms begin to fall.

Smile. Laugh. Live life. Enjoy the moment. It's all a big game anyway.

Keep a Secret

If someone trusts you enough to tell you something confidential, don't go telling about it. We all love being on the inside, having some dirt on someone, having a story about someone that is really juicy. A lot of people in business are almost overcome with a need to tell someone, anyone, everyone—this is a stupid move. Advice? Keep your mouth closed.

There are two kinds of people in my business world—those I trust and those I don't. When I hear someone telling me something I know they shouldn't, they go on my "don't tell them anything" list. They think they are creating an intimate bond with me. Stupid mistake. Obvious lesson. You talk and you never get told anything important. In business that can be a major problem.

People tell me more things than they ever should. I've got so much dirt on my competition, agents and union leaders, friends, foes—you name it, I could start my own landfill or extortion ring. But you know something? I also get insights, perceptions and personal takes on things that no one else gets. This is my reward for keeping my mouth shut.

Ego Awareness

I practiced martial arts for seven years and thought I was pretty hot by the end of my training. White boy Bruce Lee meets the Terminator. My *sensei* (teacher) could clearly see I needed a lesson in humility. The lesson? Your ego is not your friend.

One day in class he very deliberately matched me up to spar with this tiny woman about 96 pounds soaking wet. Black belt. Unhealthy gleam in her eye.

Simply put, she kicked my ass and smiled while she did it. I did not enjoy the lesson. I'm sure my *sensei* did. I sweated a gallon, turned black and blue and became the Motrin Man. She could have hurt me a lot worse.

The lesson? Never underestimate anyone based on your view of yourself. It doesn't matter how many times you've kicked butt. You put the target on your back the moment you start with the "I'm tougher than you" ego trip. Just be smarter. In retrospect, I should have asked her to coffee.

Time Allocation Analysis

Time management is being aware and focused on the utilization of your time. For you to achieve a desired result, you must mix effective strategies and time. If you have a lousy strategy, you'll chase your tail forever. If you have a great strategy but poor time management you'll end up a frustrated underachiever. As such, for the average organizer, agent or business manager this little exercise might be of use:

List the main activities that you perform every day. Not tasks, but major areas of focus. First determine the amount of time you currently spend on the area. Do this for every area of your job. Now take a look in the other column and assign percentages as they would be in an optimal or "best case" situation.

Percentage of Time Currently Spent	Activity	Optimal Percentage of Time
_____	_____	_____
_____	_____	_____
_____	_____	_____
_____	_____	_____
_____	_____	_____
_____	_____	_____

This is a very brief "vital time analysis" that will determine your effectiveness in your position. It is very rare for someone to be allocating the optimal amount of time in balance with all the responsibilities of a position. This can be influenced by the following:

- We do what we like to do.
- We don't do what we don't like to do.
- We do what we do well.
- We don't do what we are likely to fail at.
- We do what brings pleasure or avoids discomfort.
- We usually do what we've done in the past.

- We sometimes reject doing anything new.
- We won't do something additional without a reward.
- We won't do something with passion unless we understand the contribution we are making.
- We will do things that we volunteer to do.
- We won't do most anything that we are forced to do.
- We do things best where expectations are well defined.
- We do poorly at things where structure and focus are casual.
- We can always find time when we absolutely need to.
- We can always procrastinate and justify it if necessary.

Look at your allocation of time. Reallocate your time with the knowledge that comes with careful self-evaluation. Remember that your performance depends upon your time management skills.

First-Year Agent Blues

So, you are the new meat. I feel for you (after I kick you a couple of times). The members are hostile, the employers even worse. Blindly feeling your way, striving to do the best you can with what you've got. Sometimes stuck between a contract, internal politics, employers' leverage and distressed members. It is a daily tightrope. So to ask you to then go out and try to organize might seem like the final straw. Well, let me tell you, you may be the cream of the crop and not even know it.

To a new agent, the world is wide and the possibilities are endless. A new agent is ready to conquer the world, beat up the employers, take on every member's problem, make and keep promises. But over time, enthusiasm and optimism slowly give way to practicality and caution. The union agent survival instinct takes over. But the upside is that when you are new, you have no baggage and no preconceived notion of what can or cannot be done.

Many old war-horses are the worst organizers in a union stable. They are satisfied or content. They no longer have the burning desire to make the extra effort. This is not to say they do not have value—they know everyone (and figure they know everything) and can often get something done with a phone call that a new agent would have to chase his tail over for a week. But when it comes down to making call after call, trying and striving to make potential clients see the light, it takes a little bit of both.

To address first-year blues, I suggest that teams be formed that combine the best elements of the old and new. Blind ambition meets industry knowledge and history. Put the two together and the sum is greater than the parts. I do not recommend that a brand new agent be put on the street without this mentor assistance provided. As previously pointed out, you may only have one shot at a prospect and you don't want a rookie practicing on your bread and butter. He's already going to piss off lots of your existing clients. As we all know, new agents have no idea how bad they really are.

Recommended Reading

There are a couple of books I strongly suggest you read (besides this classic) to advance you on your way to business development success:

- *How to Win Friends and Influence People,* Dale Carnegie
- *What They Don't Teach You at Harvard Business School,* Mark McCormack

Two additional books I would recommend as true-life lessons in determination, leadership and willpower are:

- *Endurance,* Alfred Lansing
- *Seven Summits,* Dick Bass and Frank Wells

I would suggest that every local union require that any reps who are engaged in business development must read one book of this type every quarter. The union should follow up with small group discussions for half-day in-house seminars. Representatives should relate stories on how they succeeded in using strategies and tactics contained in the material.

Your Real Contribution

Being a labor representative can be unforgiving and harsh. I've seen it eat men alive. I've seen burnout and heartache and stress so bad guys simply had to move on. I've seen casualties of workaholism, union politics, alcohol and ambition. In these twenty years I've seen a lot. So my simple advice is to remember to take care of the most important things and people in your life first. Remember who you are. You are not what you do. Don't get lost in it. I got lost for a while. It wasn't easy to find my way back.

One hundred years from now
It will not matter
If you made business manager or
how many companies you organized,
What kind of car you drove,
What kind of house you lived in,
How much money you had,
How important you seemed in your union,
Your social circle or your community.

But one hundred years from now
The world may be a little better
Because you were important
In the life of your child.

Be a much better dad, mom, family member or friend than organizer, agent, or business manager.

CHAPTER 11

For Business Managers Only

Start by doing what's necessary,
then what's possible, and
suddenly you are doing the
impossible.
—ST. FRANCIS OF ASSISI

The Business Manager's 5 Percent

A good business manager will reserve at least five percent of his time to assist organizers. This may seem like a small portion, but five percent equals two full hours per week.

These hours should be invested in one specific way - meeting with potential clients.

There is no more effective manner in which you can determine the general business approach of any organization than by meeting with the owner or executive-in-charge. In at least 20 or 30 cases that I've been involved in, this was enough to create a profound break-through with a non-union company owner.

To have a business manager sit eye-to-eye with a prospective partner and tell him how unions have changed and how he is going to help this prospective client's business thrive is a powerful testimony.

A breakfast or lunch takes an hour. What would the impact be if a business manager did 20 or 50 or 75 such meetings per year? Five percent is actually a hell of a lot if you stick with it.

The Value of a Client

The business manager needs to tattoo this formula on the back of his hand—it is the value of a new signatory employer. When your staff members are tired of trying over and over to sign him, you may find they are undervaluing the relationship. Try reminding them of this formula:

Estimated Number of Employees Covered by the Unit

X

Annual Per Employee Dues Realized by the Union

X

Estimated Years Employer Will Remain Signatory

+

Political Clout of Additional Members

+

Reference in the Marketplace by a
Satisfied New Signatory Employee

+

Resulting Enthusiasm and Support of
Existing Union Employers

= **The Value of a New Client**

Think about this formula when you are selling the value of organizing to others in the union. It is the big picture simplified. Your agents or organizers sometimes have trouble getting motivated. It seems like too much trouble to call that prospective employer one more time. Believe me, they don't have anything more important or valuable to do right now.

Employers and Union Politics

As a business manager, you live and die by your union politics. I know how it works. I've seen it up close enough to get splattered with blood a time or two. I think it helps me to be a better negotiator and better partner. When I deal with the union, I start with the politics.

Employers do not get it. Let me repeat for this is critical— they do not get it.

For the most part, employers have little idea of the difficulties of your jobs. They don't understand the internal politics. They don't understand the international union politics. Many think you exist to hard-ass them over whining unproductive workers who are generally undeserving. They don't understand your obligation to represent every union worker in your local, whether you like them or not. Whether they deserve it or not.

So the dumb employer comes to negotiate, work with or against you and still they do not understand the most powerful influence at work from an organizational or personal standpoint.

You don't have to divulge the secrets of the union universe, but you can explain the basics. Most union leaders are miles ahead of their rank-and-file. They are leaders because they can see the big picture, but often are handcuffed by union politics from innovating or risking where it may do the most good for the industry and union members.

Help employers understand the power, influence and finality of union politics. That way, they won't be surprised when you get elected business manager. They'll know you were a politically astute, ambitious bastard and admire you for it.

Budget per New Client or Campaign

When approaching a top-down or bottom-up campaign, it is simply good business to establish a realistic estimate of anticipated costs incurred to secure the new business. Most businesses in America fully calculate ratios such as cost of sale, advertising dollars per client secured or sales calls to sales made. This level of detail is really not applicable here. However, a rough form of this type of budgeting should be standard for business managers and organizing coordinators.

A bottom-up campaign would normally include most of the following:

- Labor costs of one or more organizers over the time period necessary to contact and persuade the necessary number of workers.
- Expenses associated with election process.
- Legal expenses for challenges.
- Administrative and support overhead.
- Labor costs associated with negotiating initial collective bargaining agreement.
- Gas, travel and related expenses.

So, to secure a new client, the average cost per client ratio might be somewhere between $3,000 to $25,000 apiece, and perhaps much higher. It is unrealistic to think the total expenses will be less than $2,000 to $3,000 in labor costs alone.

A top-down campaign would normally consist of the following:

- Labor costs of one or more organizers or business managers to contact and persuade the owner or principal
- Professionally prepared presentation materials (brochures, videos, CDs, testimonials, newsletters
- Support media (optional)—testimonial advertising, marketing, public relations
- Ongoing strategic communications campaign via phone, fax, e-mail
- Labor costs associated with negotiating initial collective bargaining agreement

The cost here could be anywhere from $500 to $5,000 per client, but not less than this.

My three points are as follows:

1. The cost of securing one client is more expensive than most union leaders may think.
2. Few organizations analyze these costs against results.
3. Even fewer allocate significant resources for top-down campaigns.

If you are in a position to influence the use of money, personnel or other resources, keep these issues in mind. Make sure you track the expense ratio of business development dollars spent per new client or new union members. Use at least one year for the calculation. For newly formed programs, it is probably better to wait 18 to 24 months.

And finally, don't forget to allocate some resources for top-down campaigns. On balance, the cost per client secured is far lower.

Union Buster's Budget per Client

Professional union-busting firms (of which there is no shortage) sell all kinds of tools to the employer community to thwart your efforts. They too understand the cost-to-results ratio. It is most certainly reflected in their product and service price structure. One union busting company markets a two-video set as an instructional program to prevent unionization of the workplace. This sucker is only 52 minutes and sells for $1,449. That's 100 times the cost of this book!

Enough companies are buying it on a cost-to-results basis for it to remain a popular product. This is your competition giving you a lesson in cost-to-results marketing. To support this and other products and services, the union-busting industry must communicate a message that creates fear and apprehension in the minds of the employers. I'd say at $1,449 a pop, they are doing a damn good job of it. Are you ready to start right off spending a minimum of $1,449 per new client for the first 52 minutes of marketing?

As the underdogs or upstarts, you have to look at the resources dedicated for the result desired and shape this formula in the most cost effective and productive manner.

Addressing Stupid Contracts

If any employer really read most union contracts in fine detail, he would never sign an agreement. Sad but true. Union contracts, just like people, need to change with the times if they are to be relevant in today's marketplace.

Does your union have a stupid contract? Are you, as business manager, responsible for it or just stuck with it? If you aren't sure, then take this test.

Does your contract:

- Contain provisions that no one can really explain?
- Contain work rules that no one really enforces, they're just left over?
- Make it difficult to hire and fire?
- Have featherbedding language that you can't get rid of because of the rank-and-file?
- Have more than 100 pages?
- Restrict your employers' *ability to compete?*
- Restrict your employers' *ability to employ more of your members?*
- Restrict your employers' *ability to grow your market share?*
- Restrict your employers' *ability to recapture lost markets?*

Most of the contracts I have negotiated in the last 20 years contain sacred cow provisions that are a joke. And many of my union counterparts will (off the record) agree with me. Contracts more often reflect the old school relations that management and labor had 20 or 30 years ago as well as the market share those unions had at that time.

The reason I bring this up is that you are asking employers to become your strategic partners for a long time to come. Many labor contracts are not documents of opportunity for the future, but legacies of the past. I know that many of you will take issue with this, as much blood and sweat has been spilled over these contracts. However, sooner or later, you will have to balance the political impact of necessary contract modifications against your long-term market recovery objectives. If you've got a non-competitive agreement with leftovers from years ago, you need to know that you are pushing a big rock ahead of you as you travel down the business development path.

Backstabbing and Glory Hounding

Political infighting (mother's milk for many union knotheads) is a huge barrier to effective business development. Analyze and decide on the following before you spend one thin dime.

Political Obstacle Checklist

- Who is going to get the organizing credit and recognition?
- How will we define success?
- Does this credit reach far enough up the food chain and out to the fringes of the organization?
- Do you have an effective and ongoing organizing communication strategy aimed at your rank-and-file?
- Do you have an effective and ongoing communication strategy developed for the union employer community

that you serve (a message about evening the playing field or increasing their competitiveness)?

■ How are the organizers managed? By a centralized process exclusively focused on organizing, local by local, or other? Does anyone have a vested political interest in their failure?

■ Are family members of union leaders in the organizing department? This replicates the issues that come up in the employer family business organizational structure. Avoid resentment by making sure they can perform at higher levels than those of their peers.

Teaming Business Agents and Organizers

Often local unions do not pay enough attention to the structure of a good organizing program. The structure must take into account the fact that organizers and business agents have different jobs. It must also promote synergy between these roles for maximum positive results. Here are a few ideas to consider:

■ Agents and organizers should not be in competition.

■ Organizers should be encouraged to share the credit (like an assist in basketball) with deserving agents.

■ Agents should be encouraged to assist organizers and not worry that they are unduly taking disproportionate credit or political benefit.

■ New organizers will only be as effective as the supporting team around them. An organizer sent to a politically hostile (or even apathetic) local area is destined to under-perform his potential.

■ Training programs for each should overlap to build camaraderie and unity of purpose.

■ A connected agent can make an average organizer very successful and can help mentor superstars.

■ The same connected agent that has no "buy-in" can screw up the effort with both rank-and-file as well as the employers.

Avoiding the $100,000 Mistake

If you hire the wrong candidate for an organizer or business agent position it is going to cost your organization at least $100,000. This does not account for lost momentum, damaged relationships and permanently wrecked market opportunities.

You should implement a pre-employment evaluation in line with how other industries recruit, screen and interview applicants. Some suggestions for the process:

■ Have each job candidate interviewed by at least two top union leaders.

■ Develop standard qualifications you are looking for in the areas of communications (written and verbal), leadership and decision making.

■ Have each candidate interviewed by a team of three of the best organizers in the region. Have their evaluations made independently from each other, in writing—you know the old saying, "it takes one to know one."

- Ask questions that have real life scenarios built in and ask what they would do or how they would react. Almost all fire and police departments use this type of interview to build teams that will be cohesive and effective under stress.

- Do it every time for every candidate. I know this sounds quite anti-union in nature, but if you pick the wrong individual for the job, remember it will probably cost at least $100,000 minimum before you change horses.

Rules for Organizer Training

Rule #1–Develop a basic training curriculum. If you don't have one, then beg, borrow or steal one from another union or use resources (such as myself) to develop one for you. Imagine trying to train apprentices with no curriculum.

Rule #2–Set up a training period duration. An apprentice does not have the technical skills or productivity of a journeyman in any craft. Why would it be any different with new business agents or organizers? Set a training program with benchmarks for skill development and productivity that are at 1,000-hour intervals over a two-year period.

Rule #3–Invest in organizer training. Basic areas of focus for this training would include:

- Time management
- Communications
- Sales and marketing
- Negotiations
- Dealing with difficult people
- Business writing

Assessing Performers and Pretenders

This is not "Big Brother" talking here but people get real weird when they consider personality-assessment models. Let me tell you, these are excellent programs for personnel evaluation. There is no better way to get someone to perform better than to provide them with insightful information (that the organizer or agent recognizes as accurate and legitimate) on their own tendencies and abilities, both positive and negative. For the boss, it provides the inside scoop on how to best manage your key players.

The most widely used and proven assessment model is the DISC. I have used this in my association for the past fifteen years. My use has been limited to a group meeting every two years with a full DISC evaluation program for each of my employees. The employees always are amazed to find the tests 95 to 98 percent accurate. This type of program would provide the following benefits in a union environment:

- An excellent analysis of how to approach (persuade) various personality types
- Illustrations that show many problems in the workplace are not personal as much as differences in personal style
- A very accurate picture for agents and organizers of their strengths and vulnerabilities
- An essential condensed curriculum on human psychology in one day that can be put to work the next week

Just so you know, the assessments do not contain invasive or personal questions. They are not like the tests given by some corporations to test honesty or other characteristics. They contain no information that could be used against someone in a personal or professional manner. They are used in thousands of businesses and executive development programs around the United States every year. Many are offered on-line. Try one yourself and see if the benefit is not self-evident.

Incentive Programs and Rewards

Incentives are a great component for any business development program. It answers the basic question of "Why should I do this?" Sure, organizing and business development are inherently part of the job, but "Why do *more* when it's so hard to do, and it's so easy to just keep doing what I've always done?" Incentives come in three forms—group rewards and recognition, individual rewards and recognition and star player rewards and recognition.

Group rewards are given to everyone who participates in an effort that meets a goal. Let's say the union establishes a goal of 10 new companies in a quarter. Those who participate in this group effort are recognized or rewarded. Some unions I have worked with have established permanent plaques for this purpose by recognizing the Local of the Month, Quarter or Year. Recognition is usually the best method to reward groups.

Individual awards should be provided to producers. These producers should be given something in front of their peers. I suggest personalized jackets, belt buckles, plaques, trophies, sports tickets or related items. This will get the competitive juices flowing. The producers will be proud and even more highly motivated. Those who have not gotten on the bandwagon might consider their options.

And finally, the star player rewards. It is a fact that 80 percent of sales are made by 5 to10 percent of a sales force. There is no reason to believe it will be any different in your union. Thus, the big closers, the killer-instinct go-getters need to be shooting for something big—really big. One union that I have worked with provides a trip for two to Hawaii for the top producer. At the end of the year, the top three or four guys are out there killing themselves to bring in new clients. It pays for itself several times over. This is no different from other businesses in America. Over a billion dollars a year is spent by American business on "incentive travel," where top performers earn or win some great trip due to their performance. Why should unions ignore this powerful and universally popular strategy? Remember, no one does anything unless it's basically in line with his or her interests. Rewards, recognition and incentives boost that interest and make things happen.

Mixing Up Approach Teams

You may find that some union reps are better at communicating with rank-and-file, while others are better with the employer prospects. Don't be afraid to mix and match by talent, rather than dealing with strict geographic restrictions on who talks to who. Sometimes a creative team approach kills two birds with one stone—bringing home the contract and also creating cooperation among individuals who usually could care less about (or perhaps are openly hostile towards) each other.

Consider giving greater recognition, incentives or rewards to those who help others recruit or organize outside of their direct areas. It's kind of like the assists or rebound statistics in sports—it may not be the direct score, but it helps the team win the game.

Involving Other Crafts

This is a tricky one. It might seem like a good idea to have the union brotherhood all organizing together, especially if the crafts are going to be working together on the project, job site or facility. *But* (isn't there always a but?), I do not recommend it.

I have yet to see two unions work in a complementary manner on a business development issue. Kind of like two dogs eyeing the same bone; it is highly unlikely that it will be shared equally. It's usually a small and seemingly insignificant issue that suddenly becomes a major obstacle, argument or pissing contest.

More than one union does not work. It's a great concept with an inevitable result: poor execution. Be a mercenary, go it alone and let someone else coattail on your success.

CHAPTER 12

Summary: An Army of One

A wise man will make more opportunities than he finds.
—SIR FRANCIS BACON

One Guy, One Company, One Year at a Time

Now has come the moment of truth.

Do the concepts in this book make sense? Are they relevant to labor's strategic approach to future business development or are they just foolish ramblings of a management S.O.B.?

For what it is worth, I believe this approach, combined with meeting your clients' needs, can recapture 20 to 50 percent of the market that you have lost. Yes, that means that there is still somewhere between 50 to 80 percent that you will either have to organize bottom-up or write off forever. But still, the market that you can recover utilizing these concepts represents thousands of employers and probably hundreds of thousands of workers.

The power of this approach can pay surprising dividends as the following story might illustrate.

I began my "organizing" in 1995. Since that time I have facilitated union relationships for approximately 100 non-union firms. This was on a very part-time basis. These non-union companies ranged from mom-and-pop companies to firms doing over $25 million per year. To illustrate the power of patience and time, I did a little math on my efforts and came up with the following rather surprising conclusions:

Those 100 companies (now unionized) multiplied by an annual construction volume of $3 million per year (a low estimate) now equal $300 million in union contract dollars per year!

I'd estimate that the average duration of affiliation for a union contractor is probably about 15 years. Let's multiply 15 years x $300 million per year for a total of $4.5 *billion* in union contract volume for these 100 organized companies while they are in business.

Let's figure labor costs at roughly 30 percent of any job. Take 30 percent of the $4.5 billion construction volume total and calculate it to be about $1.5 billion in labor wages and fringe benefits paid by these 100 companies.

If the average rank-and-file guy gets 1,500 hours at a total wage and fringe benefit package of $40 per hour, the total is about $60,000 per year. Divide $60,000 into the $1.5 billion paid to the workers and the trust funds. This equals an astounding 25,000 union man years paid to workers and trust funds and $4.5 billion in unionized construction contracts.

And that is if I never sign one more company. And I'm only one guy. An army of one. And so are you.

What Are You Gonna Do Now?

From my irrelevant management viewpoint, the rest is up to you. I have shared with you my best effort. Therefore, you are now burdened with the knowledge that I have shared and you have to figure out what to do with it. I'd like to finish with some options just so you know I haven't gone soft on you.

Option 1: Ignore all of it. Run against the progressive business manager. Condemn him for loving scabs and rats. Win on a hardball ticket, lose all your market share and go down as the last and worst business manager ever.

Option 2: Try a little at a time. Plant seeds and watch them grow. Identify the guys that get it and give them the tools they need. Take most of the credit but don't be an asshole about it.

Option 3: Pull out all the stops. Rage against the political obstacles. Tell the old guard to shut their f**king traps because if they really knew what was up, the results would show it. Get a bunch of young lions and start eating your way to the top. Do not accept the status quo ever again.

Option 4: Sit quietly and think of one good thing you can use every day. Do it and don't tell anyone. Build on it. Be satisfied to see it work. Enjoy your job, life, family and accomplishments just a little bit more.

And then give this book to another guy who you know needs it.

About the Author

Mark Breslin is the fourth generation of a construction family. His great grandfather, grandfather and stepfather were all contractors.

He has served as the Executive Director of the Engineering and Utility Contractors Association for nearly 20 years. The association is a multi-employer bargaining organization that represents union construction firms in California doing billions of dollars in contracts each year. Mark became the chief executive and director at age 26. He has served in this capacity as chief negotiator and contractor advocate.

As a professional speaker, trainer and facilitator he has spoken to more than 50,000 business and labor leaders around the United States and Canada. He is the leading speaker in the nation on business development and marketing strategies for labor and management.

He graduated from San Francisco State University with a BA in Industrial Design. He has since taught labor relations and human resource management at Golden Gate and Sonoma State Universities.

Mark lives in northern California with his wife Susan and their three children. When not provoking labor leaders, his real life passions include mountaineering and expedition travel. Recent challenges include summiting Mt. Rainier, trekking in the Sahara, and raising teenagers.

127

Change Our Industry
with books by Mark Breslin

CHECK **www.breslin.biz** *OR ORDER HERE*

Qty	TITLE	PRICE EACH	Sales tax CA res. only	TOTAL DUE
	Organize or Die *(book)*	$19.95	1.66 ea	
	Organize or Die audio CD *(2-CD set, 3 hours)*	34.95	2.90 ea	
	Survival of the Fittest *(book)*	19.95	1.66 ea	
	Survival of the Fittest Workbook and Discussion Guide	14.95	1.24 ea	
	Survival of the Fittest Apprentice and Training Instructor's Guide	29.95	2.49 ea	
	Survival of the Fittest audio CD *(2-CD set)*	24.95	2.07 ea	
	Survival of the Fittest DVD	149.95	12.45ea	
	Survival of the Fittest Training Pack	193.00	16.02ea	
	SHIPPING: $2.95 per item*	____ items x $2.95 =		

*FREE SHIPPING when ordering 50 items or more.
Canadian orders must be accompanied by a postal money order in U.S. funds.
Allow 15 days for delivery. Call 866-351-6275 for quantity discounts.

❑ **YES**, I am interested in having Mark Breslin speak or give a seminar to my training center, local union, company, building trades or association. Please send information.

My check or money order for $_____ is enclosed.

Name _____

Organization _____

Address _____

City/State/Zip _____

Phone_____ E-mail _____

Please make your check payable and return to:

Breslin Strategies, Inc. c/o McAlly International Press
2415 San Ramon Valley Blvd, #4-230 • San Ramon, CA 94583
or visit **www.breslin.biz** *to charge your purchase*